CAREERS FOR

INTROVERTS

& Other Solitary Types

Careers for You Series

CAREERS FOR

INTROVERTS

& Other Solitary Types

BLYTHE CAMENSON

SECOND EDITION

McGraw·Hill

New York   Chicago   San Francisco   Lisbon   London   Madrid   Mexico City
Milan   New Delhi   San Juan   Seoul   Singapore   Sydney   Toronto

Library of Congress Cataloging-in-Publication Data

Camenson, Blythe.
    Careers for introverts & other solitary types / by Blythe Camenson — 2nd ed.
      p. cm. — (McGraw-Hill careers for you series)
    ISBN 0-07-144861-6 (alk. paper)
      1. Vocational guidance—United States.   2. Introversion.   I. Title: Careers
for introverts and other solitary types.   II. Title.   III. Series.

    HF5382.5.U5C2518 2006
    331.702'0973—dc22   2005004474

1 2 3 4 5 6 7 8 9 0   DOC/DOC   0 9 8 7 6 5

ISBN 0-07-144861-6

McGraw-Hill books are available at special quantity discounts to use as premiums and
sales promotions, or for use in corporate training programs. For more information,
please write to the Director of Special Sales, Professional Publishing, McGraw-Hill,
Two Penn Plaza, New York, NY 10121-2298. Or contact your local bookstore.

This book is printed on acid-free paper.

Contents

Acknowledgments

··

The author would like to thank the following professionals for providing information about their careers:

Jim Anderson, Stained-Glass Artist
Patricia Baker, Costumer
Susan Broadwater-Chen, Information Specialist
Robyn Carr, Novelist
Nick Delia, Letter Carrier
John Fleckner, Archivist
Tom Gerhardt, Cooper
Jan Goldberg, Author and Freelance Writer
Jim Haskins, Biographer
Deb Mason, Potter
Ronald Miller, Conservation Specialist
Stephen Morrill, Online Instructor
Valarie Neiman, Researcher
Carol Perry, Travel Writer
Peggy Peters, Freelance Illustrator
Joel Pontz, Joiner
Rosalind Sedacca, Advertising Copywriter
Timothy J. Speed Jr., Security Supervisor

The editors wish to acknowledge Josephine Scanlon for revising this second edition.

CHAPTER ONE

Careers for Introverts

Perhaps you consider yourself an introvert—you're shy. Or maybe you just prefer to be independent, allowed to work on your own without having to answer to a boss or deal with a lot of different people. You're more comfortable working with things or ideas than with customers or clients. You're happiest when you're working alone.

Although almost every job out there involves at least some minimal contact with other people, there is a wide range of careers for those of you who prefer to go it solo.

In *Careers for Introverts* you will find a selection of professions with a variety of background and training requirements, but they all have one common thread: they're ideal for the autonomous individualist.

Choosing Your Field

People involved with independent work give of themselves in many different capacities, providing a variety of valuable services. If you're reading this book, chances are you're already considering a career in one of the many areas of this wide-open occupational category.

But perhaps you're not sure of the working conditions the different fields offer or which area would best suit your personality, skills, and lifestyle. There are several factors to consider when deciding which sector to pursue. Each field carries with it different levels of responsibility and commitment. To identify occupations that will match your expectations, you need to know what each job entails.

Ask yourself the following questions and make note of your answers. Then, as you go through the following chapters, compare your requirements to the information provided by the professionals interviewed. Their comments will help you pinpoint the fields that interest you and eliminate those that clearly would be the wrong choice.

- How much time are you willing to commit to training? Some skills can be learned on the job or in a year or two of formal training; others can take considerably longer.
- Do you want to work behind a desk in a home office, or would you prefer to be out and about working alone in parks or forests or even delivering the mail?
- Can you handle a certain amount of stress on the job, or would you prefer a self-paced workload?
- How much money do you expect to earn starting out and after you have a few years' experience under your belt? Salaries and earnings vary greatly in each chosen profession.
- How much independence do you require? Do you want to work alone, or will you be comfortable with varying degrees of contact with coworkers, supervisors, or clients?

Knowing what your expectations are and then comparing them to the realities of the work will help you make informed choices.

Ideal Careers for Introverts

Writers

Writers are well known for working alone. Nothing can stop the creative flow more for a writer than the sound of a phone ringing or another human voice. Full-time writers sit by themselves at their computers for hours a day. And though, just as with artists, they need other people to sell their work, most contacts can be handled through the mail. An agent's phone call to report a sale is the only welcome interruption.

Artists

Perhaps no other endeavor conjures an image of solo workers better than that of talented artists, struggling by themselves in a studio (or garret) with nothing for companionship other than a radio and the smell of linseed oil and paint. While it's true that some artists use models, many others work with props or from memory. And though at some point most studio and commercial artists might have to venture out among people to sell their work, most of their time is spent in solitary creation.

Researchers

Would your ideal job allow you to keep your nose in a book or scan the thousands of sites on the Internet? If so, then a freelance research position might be the career for you.

Archivists

Archivists work with documents that are preserved for use by researchers and others interested in historical information. If you are interested in organizing and documenting the past, a career as an archivist might be right for you.

Computer Professionals

Computer professionals may pursue a variety of career paths, and many of these involve working independently. From systems analyst to online instructor, there are nearly as many career titles as there are people interested in this field.

Forest Rangers

Picture yourself in a pristine forest, where the only sounds are the wind blowing through the trees and the rustle of leaves as small creatures scamper by. In national parks and forests, rangers are hired to watch for fires and protect against unlawful hunting or logging or any disturbances, human or otherwise, that would upset the balance of nature. Park rangers also work with people to some extent, functioning as guides or interpretative rangers.

Security Guards

Security guards, and most often nighttime security officers, have lonely and sometimes boring jobs. It's not a career for anyone but the introverted type who enjoys quiet and solitude. But introverts working as security guards also have to be prepared for intrusions. After all, they are hired to look out for trespassers, vandals, or other criminals, and though a quiet shift is the ideal, sometimes the work pace is anything but.

Mail Carriers

Each day, the U.S. Postal Service receives, sorts, and delivers millions of letters, bills, advertisements, and packages. To do this, it employs about 845,000 workers. Almost half of these workers are postal clerks, who sort mail and serve customers in post offices, or mail carriers, who deliver the mail.

Although mail carriers spend some time each day at the post office, collecting the mail for their routes and interacting with coworkers and supervisors, much of their time is spent working independently as they make their deliveries.

The Qualifications You'll Need

Because the careers for independent types vary so greatly, understandably the requirements and qualifications for employment also vary. More and more professional positions require at least a bachelor's degree. However, some of the careers highlighted here require applicants to have certain specialized skills rather than diplomas.

Table 1 lists many of the careers featured in the following pages. Pinpoint the job that interests you, then look to the right to find the education or training requirements. Each job's prerequisites will be covered more fully in the chapters ahead.

TABLE I. Education Requirements					
JOB TITLE	**HS**	**B.A./B.S.**	**M.A./M.S.**	**PH.D.**	**OTHER**
Writers					X
Artists		X^P			X
Researchers		X	X^P		
Archivists			X^R	X^P	
Computer Professionals		X^R	X^P		
Security Guards	X				
Forest Rangers		X^R			
Mail Carriers	X				
P=Preferred	R=Required				

Salaries

Just as the required qualifications differ, so do salaries. How much you'll earn will depend on your work setting, your employer, and your level of education and training, as well as the geographic area in which you live. Throughout the following chapters you will learn more about the specific salaries that professionals in each featured career can expect to draw.

For More Information

In the Appendix you will find professional associations for many of the career paths explored in this book. Most offer valuable information about the careers at their websites, and many provide links to other helpful resources.

CHAPTER TWO

Writers

Although writers come from all sorts of backgrounds and are as different as one person is from the next, they do have a few things in common. For one thing, they are more than comfortable working alone. In fact, for most writers, solitude is a necessity.

Writers also share a love of words. They love how words sound and how they fit together in original and rhythmic ways. They love playing with an idea and letting it grow until it becomes a workable magazine article, advertisement, story, novel, or nonfiction book.

They love seeing the words fill their computer screens and print in neat lines on what was once a blank sheet of paper. They love the sense of accomplishment they feel when a project has been completed, when it satisfies a client or finds a home in a book or magazine.

They love seeing their names in print, giving them credit for their writing, and they love receiving the checks, which in essence say "thanks for a job well done."

However, there are frustrations and disappointments, too. Becoming a professional writer is not an easy task. New writers face stiff competition from experienced writers with proven track records. Impersonal rejection slips become a way of life for new writers, who sometimes must wonder if they have a better chance at winning the lottery than getting published.

But new writers do get published every year. It takes persistence, skill, knowledge of the trade, and a little luck, but if it's what you want more than anything else, you can make it happen.

In this chapter we will cover many different writing careers and explore how you can get started. You will also meet several successful writers and learn what the writing life is like for them.

Novelists

Fiction writers are creative, imaginative people. After all, they have to be; they make up stories for a living. Whether writing short stories or full-length novels, fiction writers have to be able to create imaginary characters and events and make them seem real to their readers.

Fiction writers have to be troublemakers, too, inventing all sorts of problems for their characters. They have to make their conversations and thoughts entertaining and fill their characters' lives with action. Finally, fiction writers have to be expert problem solvers, helping their heroes find satisfying solutions to their troubles by the end of the story.

If you love to read fiction and you find yourself stopping in the middle of a book and saying out loud, "I could do that better," then maybe you can.

The Novelist's Life

Few new fiction writers have the luxury of working at their craft full-time. Most need to maintain some other sort of employment to help pay the bills until they are able to support themselves through their writing. Because of this, dedicated writers use every spare minute they have to work on their books or stories. John Grisham, for example, wrote a good deal of *The Firm* on yellow legal pads while taking the train to and from work as a full-time attorney in a law firm. Others get up an hour early, stay up an hour late, turn down invitations to parties or other social events, or let the housework go—whatever they can do to find the time to write.

Successful authors who support themselves through their writing treat it as a full-time job. Most report learning how to discipline themselves to put in a certain number of hours each day.

Every writer chooses a schedule that is comfortable. Some work in the early hours of the morning, take afternoon naps, then go back to the computer in the evenings. Others write for eight or ten or twelve hours straight each day for a period of months until the book is finished. Still others might take years to complete one volume.

There is no set formula for how a writer should work. The only rule is that you have to write. Author James Clavell said that even if you write only one page every day for a year, at the end of that time you'll have 365 pages. And that's a substantial book.

The Many Categories of Fiction

Next time you visit a bookstore, take note of where the different books are shelved and what the signs in each section say. Here is an example of some of the different genres or categories you'll encounter, along with a few of their subgenres.

General/Mainstream
Action/Adventure
Children's
Fantasy
Historical
Horror
Literary
Science Fiction
Mystery
  Cozy
  Crime
  Detective
  Police Procedural

Romance
  Contemporary
  Historical
    Gothic
    Regencies
  Sensuous
  Sweet
Suspense
  Psychological
  Thriller
Western
Young Adult

How to Submit Your Work

Writing a novel or short story is only half the battle. The next challenge is knowing how to submit your work for publication. Your manuscript must be typed in a format acceptable to an editor. *Writer's Market*, an annual publication from Writer's Digest Books, offers valuable information on all aspects of manuscript preparation and submission.

In the past, a novice author could submit a manuscript directly to an editor in the hope that he or she would read the book and buy it. The writer could negotiate the contract or use the sale to get an agent. Times have changed, however. Editors no longer have the time to read books that come in "over the transom." If a publisher does accept such submissions, it is possible that they are read by less experienced assistants rather than by editors. Some small presses do still consider work submitted directly by an author, but if you are interested in submitting your manuscript to a major publisher, you will almost definitely need an agent.

It is important to note that many publishers no longer accept unsolicited manuscripts or those that are not sent through an agent. Submission by an agent offers an implicit statement that the book has been read and judged good enough to consider for publication. An agent should also know which editor is the best choice for your work. *Writer's Market* and the Association of Authors' Representatives both offer helpful tips for finding an agent.

An agent typically receives a commission of 15 percent of the book sale. While this might seem like a high percentage to a fledgling writer, bear in mind that an agent is also experienced in negotiating contracts and will probably get you a much better deal than you would be able to negotiate on your own.

The Rewards, the Pay, the Perks

Few new fiction writers have the luxury of working at their craft full-time. Most need to maintain some other sort of employment to help pay the bills until they are able to support themselves through their writing.

Even if you manage to break in and sell your first novel, you should expect to receive an advance of about five thousand dollars. The six-figure advances that some superstar authors receive are not the norm. John Scognamiglio, an editor at Kensington Publishing, says, "That kind of stuff like with John Grisham doesn't really have anything to do with the rest of us. There are 110,000 new titles a year, and there are only 15 on the *New York Times* bestseller list at a time. Most of the rest of us are going to make a moderate income and do a civilized business if we work very, very hard. There's not that much room at the top. And there isn't much of a middle class in publishing. You either make a little bit of money, which the grand majority will do, or you make a lot."

If you do manage to land that first book contract, you will receive an advance against royalties. A royalty is a percentage, usually 6 to 10 percent, of the money your book earns in sales. The advance is usually paid half on signing the contract and half on acceptance of the completed manuscript.

What It's Really Like

Read the following account of a successful novelist to see whether this might be the career for you.

Robyn Carr, Novelist

Robyn Carr has written twenty books since 1980. Her first twelve novels are in the historical or category romance genre. But in 1992, Robyn switched genres and wrote *Mind Tryst*, a psychological suspense/thriller published by St. Martin's Press. Her most recent novel is *Blue Skies*, published by MIRA Books in 2004. In addition to writing novels, Robyn has taught for the Writer's Digest School of Writing and is the author of *Practical Tips for Writing Popular Fiction* (Writer's Digest Books).

How Robyn Started Writing. Robyn describes her start as a writer as rather unexceptional: "I'm a very ordinary person. While

I was pregnant I read a lot and thought anybody with half a brain could do this, which is how everyone thinks in the beginning. You write that first book and you're sure it's going to be *Gone with the Wind*, but it's really junk. But something happens to you when you're doing it. It held my interest to the point that it became an obsessive desire to write. I couldn't wait to get back to it."

Robyn Carr's first sale was through an agent. She had made previous submissions on her own, but the agent sent her manuscript to thirteen publishers. After twelve rejections, Little, Brown and Company bought the novel, *Chelynne*, which was published in 1980.

Taking a New Direction. Robyn decided to switch from writing romance novels after feeling that "I was getting burned out. It was hard to find anything new." She enjoys her new genre, saying, "I'm not tired of suspense—it's like traveling . . . and who knows where I'll go next."

Constructing the Plot. Constructing the plot is very important in a suspense novel, especially since so much rests on when certain discoveries are made. In order to build suspense, the author has to remember many details. Robyn makes plot outlines on index cards that she can lay out on a table and move around. This helps her to arrange elements of the plot and to decide when to introduce certain information to the reader. She also has other people read her manuscripts before submission to be sure that she has not left any loose ends in the plot.

Many of us, both avid readers and aspiring authors, wonder about the writing process. Does an author write the story from start to finish, prepare an outline from which to flesh out the plot, or continually revise throughout the writing? Robyn's advice, which is shared by many professional writers, is to outline, write the story through, and then revise.

Robyn always has a clear idea of what will happen in her books before she begins writing. Some minor details might change along the way, but the basic premise remains solid. Her characters' personalities develop during the writing process, as she feels more comfortable giving them specific attributes and emotions. It usually is not until she has completed a novel that Robyn is fully clear on just what her characters' personalities really are.

Advice from Robyn Carr. Robyn offers a few tips for writing suspense novels:

* Don't confuse building suspense with withholding information. The opposite is true; the more information you give, the more suspense you build.
* Keeping secrets from the reader breaks a hard-and-fast rule. The reader has to know everything the main character knows. The character, from whose point of view the story is told, can't hide thoughts from the reader.
* Remember that the reader is entitled to an equal opportunity to solve the mystery along with your characters.

Freelance Writers

A freelance writer works independently, in a rented office space or in a home office. Most freelance writers plan and write articles and columns on their own and actively seek out new markets in which to place them.

Many freelancers start out working as staff writers at magazines or other publications until they establish themselves; others set up shop in a home office right away, selling their work to publishers or different kinds of publications, manufacturing firms, and public relations and advertising departments or agencies. They sometimes contract to complete specific assignments, such as writing about a new product or technique. There are many people—business owners or politicians, for example—who hire the services of professional writers to do their writing for them because they lack either the skill or the time.

Freelancers can keep busy writing magazine ads, travel brochures, political speeches, or press releases. The possibilities are as varied as the number of clients a writer can develop.

What the Work Involves

Freelancers can take on a variety of roles as writers. Here are four examples.

1. **Advertising copywriters** write all the words for magazine ads and radio and TV commercials. To describe a business's services or a client's products, they write the copy for brochures or pamphlets. They write all the copy for direct-mail packages, which are used to sell products or services, such as magazine subscriptions or book club memberships, through the mail.

2. **Ghostwriters** write books for people who don't have the necessary skill to do it themselves. The client could be a famous person, such as a former president or a movie star, who has a story to tell but needs help telling it. Ghostwriters sometimes get credit for their writing (you might see "as told to" on the book jacket cover), but often they remain anonymous, writing behind the scenes.

3. **Press secretaries** work for government officials, actors, or big corporations that are concerned with relations with the press. They schedule public appearances and read prepared statements to reporters. They also write press releases, which are announcements of events, services, or products. Press releases are sent to various newspapers and TV and radio shows in the hope of receiving some free publicity.

4. **Speech writers** work with politicians and other public figures, listening to what they want to say, then writing the speeches they will deliver. When you listen to the president on television or see the mayor or governor speaking to a group of voters, you can make a good bet that the speech was written by someone else.

Finding Clients

Many writers work for ad agencies, gaining experience and making contacts before striking out on their own. Others might start with just one client, a big corporation, for example, that will send enough work their way. And, through building a reputation as a good worker who delivers on time, a freelancer receives recommendations that lead to new clients. Word of mouth is how most writers build up business.

The Rewards, the Pay, the Perks

In many careers, especially in the various areas of the writing profession, you'll hear the expression "the work is its own reward." What that means is the money you make doing that work isn't

TABLE 1. Sample Freelance Writing Fees

	HOURLY	PER PROJECT
Advertising copywriting	$20–$100	$200–$4,000
Book-jacket copywriting	$100–$600	
Brochures	$20–$50	$200–$4,000
Business catalogs	$25–$40	$60–$75/printed page
Direct-mail package		$1,500–$10,000
Encyclopedia articles		$60–$80/1,000 words
Ghostwriting	$25–$100	$400–$25,000 or 100% of the advance and 50% of royalties
Greeting cards		$20–$200 per verse
Press kits		$500–$3,000
Press releases		$80–$300
Speech writing	$20–$75	$100–$5,000 (depending on the client)
Technical writing	$35–$75	$5/page

particularly exciting. But in the case of writing for others, the money can be as rewarding as the work.

Most people who write for others do it on a freelance basis. Although some charge a flat hourly rate, most charge by the project. It can be feast or famine starting out, but once you build a steady client base, your income can be very attractive.

Writers who do earn straight salaries work for magazines, newspapers, advertising agencies, and public relations firms. Salaries can range from less than twenty thousand dollars a year for entry-level positions all the way up to seventy-five thousand dollars or more for experienced and successful employees.

Table 1 shows some examples of what freelancers charge for a few selected projects. These figures are averages; amounts vary according to the size and scope of the project, the client's industry, and the geographic region.

The Pleasures and Pressures of Freelance Writing

Independence is one of the pluses freelancers cite when asked about their work. For many jobs or projects, you can do your work in a home office, delivering the project when it's finished. You choose the projects you want to work on, and you set your own salary or fees.

The downside is that you have to learn how to promote yourself and seek out clients. In the beginning you might have to call strangers on the phone or knock on office doors looking for work.

When you do have work, you'll also have deadlines. This means you'll have to deliver on time.

And some writers have a hard time asking for money. They would love to leave the business end of things to someone else. But when you write for others, you have to wear all the different hats. It's up to you to set the fee, draw up the invoices, and bill the client. It's also up to you to collect from the client if he or she happens to be late or seems as if he or she might not pay at all.

What It's Really Like

If you think working as a freelance writer might be appealing, read on to see whether you are cut out for this interesting work.

Rosalind Sedacca, Advertising Copywriter

Rosalind Sedacca is a business communications strategist whose experience includes over twenty years as an award-winning advertising copywriter. She has written advertising copy for brochures, magazine ads, and television commercials. Rosalind believes that it's important to always meet deadlines and to always give clients a little more than they're asking for. It's important that they feel they're getting their money's worth.

How Rosalind Got Started. Rosalind's career began right after college, in the advertising department of *Vogue* magazine. She worked as an assistant to the person who wrote subscription letters, and a year later she became creative director of circulation promotion for Condé Nast Publications, which owns *Vogue*, *Glamour*, *Mademoiselle*, *House and Garden*, and *Brides* magazines. "It was a pretty cushy job for someone who was twenty-one years old," she says. "It inadvertently made me a direct-mail/advertising expert. I was with them for two years, then I left and moved into more general advertising for various advertising agencies in New York City, St. Louis, and Nashville. In 1984, I went out on my own, and I've been independent since then."

The Role of an Advertising Copywriter. Rosalind describes her work as writing ads for magazines, television and radio commercials, brochures, direct-mail packages, video scripts, newsletters, sales letters, and any other kind of material that needs to be written to help a company sell its product.

"When you write an ad, the first thing you have to know is what the purpose is," Rosalind says. "Then you want to understand who the market is, who will eventually be reading your writing. You have to understand the demographics—their age, their background, their sex, their income, their education level, and their interests.

"If I'm writing a print ad for a teenage audience, I'm going to write it a lot differently from an ad for mothers or engineers."

Rosalind works with graphic designers who handle the art and layout for a project. Together they brainstorm to come up with the best campaign, one that combines the words and the art to the best advantage of the product.

"The goal is to get people to visit, to buy, to subscribe, or to join," she says. "The products I write copy for include computers, hotels and resorts such as Club Med, banks and real-estate companies, car and appliance manufacturers, museums, magazines—all sorts of things."

One of the most interesting projects Rosalind has ever worked on is a new invention designed to detect counterfeit products. "There are so many forgeries in the world; it's become an international crisis. Unsuspecting buyers, thinking they are purchasing real Rolex watches or Reebok shoes, for example, might end up with very good fakes. Counterfeiters also print fake tickets for sporting events or theater shows, or fake money from countries around the world."

Rosalind's client is the inventor of a device that will help stop this counterfeiting. He has created a plastic decoder that, when placed over a plastic strip on the product, will show if it's genuine or not. Manufacturers can travel to different flea markets and shops to check for fake products.

When the device is in place, they'll be able to read the words, "Genuine Reeboks" or "Genuine Currency." If those words don't appear, the manufacturers will know their products have been copied. Rosalind's job was to write a detailed brochure describing this new invention and to help set up a promotional tour for the client.

The Upside of the Job. Rosalind describes her work as stimulating and creative. "I never get bored; no two days are ever the same," she says. "What I like best, and what also can be a challenge, is that one minute I'm writing about a hotel, and the next minute I'm writing about a computer, and then I'm turning around and writing about a bank or about shoes. Sometimes it's hard to change mental gears to focus from one topic to another. It's the plus and the minus together.

"But I've got a perfect mix. Part of the week I'm in my home office working at the computer. I don't have to get dressed; no one sees me. I'm just on the phone a lot. The other part of the week I'm in meetings, either developing new clients or delivering my work, and then I'm dressed to the hilt and showing myself as a professional.

The Downside. "The phone can take up a lot of my time, and I have to wear many hats. I do my own accounting and taxes, filing, all that administrative work, such as sending bills to clients. I'd much rather be writing, but in a small business you have to do everything.

"And when you start out, the finances can be tricky at first. Feast or famine. But now it's smoothed out for me; I've been in business for a long time."

Writing for Magazines

Visit any bookstore or newsstand and you will see hundreds of publications covering a variety of topics—from sports and cars to fashion and parenting. There are also many you won't see there: the hundreds of trade journals and magazines written for businesses, industries, and professional workers in as many different careers.

These publications all offer information on diverse subjects to their equally diverse readership. They are filled with articles and profiles, interviews and editorials, letters and advice, as well as pages and pages of advertisements. But without writers there would be nothing but advertisements between their covers—and even those are produced by writers!

Whether you work for a magazine full-time or as an independent freelancer, you will discover there is no shortage of markets where you can find work or sell your articles.

Staff Writers vs. Freelancers

A staff writer is employed full-time by a publication. She or he comes into work every day and is given article assignments to research and write or works with an editor to develop ideas.

A freelance writer works independently, in rented office space or in a home office. Most freelance writers plan and write articles and columns on their own and actively seek out new markets in which to place them.

Staff writers might have less freedom in choosing what to write, but they generally have more job security and always know when the next paycheck will arrive. Freelancers trade job security and regular pay for independence.

Both freelancers and those permanently employed have to produce high-quality work. They have editors to report to and deadlines to meet.

Staff writers sometimes start out as editorial assistants and show their talents while on the job, leading them into a promotion. But to get a full-time, permanent position or regular assignments from a publication, writers must be able to show a successful track record and a portfolio of published clips showcasing their best work.

Different Kinds of Articles

Articles fall into two broad categories: those that educate and those that entertain. Here is just a small sampling of the topics magazine articles cover.

Art	Hobbies
Aviation	Humor
Business and finance	Military
Careers	Nature
Child care	Pets
Computers	Photography
Contemporary culture	Politics
Entertainment	Psychology and self-help
Food	Retirement
Gardening	Science
General interest	Sports
Health	Travel

Although the subject matter can be very different, most magazine articles include many of the same elements. They all start with an interesting "hook," that first paragraph that grabs the reader's (and the editor's) attention. They use quotes from real people, mention important facts, and sometimes include amusing anecdotes or experiences.

Getting That First Article Published

Freelance writers don't need long, impressive resumes to sell their first article. Good writing will speak for itself.

Before starting, read as many magazines as you can, and in particular those you would like to write for. It's never a good idea to send an article to a magazine you have never seen before. Being familiar with the different magazines will also help you come up with future article ideas.

Once you have decided what you want to write about, there are two ways you can go. You can write the entire article "on spec," sending it off to appropriate editors and hoping they like your topic. Or first you can write a query letter, a kind of miniproposal, to see if there is any interest in your idea. Query letters will save you the time of writing articles you might have difficulty selling.

Only once you're given a definite assignment do you then proceed. If you are sending a query letter, you might want to include "clips," or samples of previously published articles, especially if you have something on a similar topic.

There are three important keys to keep in mind to get your articles published:

1. Make sure your writing is polished and that your article includes all the important elements.
2. Make sure your letter and manuscript are neatly typed and free of mistakes.
3. Make sure you are sending your article to the right publication. A magazine that features stories only on planning the perfect wedding will not be interested in your piece on ten tips for the perfect divorce.

You can learn more out about different magazines and the kinds of material they prefer to publish in the market guides listed in the Appendix.

The Rewards, the Pay, the Perks

Most writers are thrilled to see their "byline," that is, their name on the page, giving them credit for the article. And to writers, nothing is more exciting than the finished product—the article in print. Receiving a check or a salary for your efforts can be rewarding as well, but unfortunately for new freelancers, the checks might not come often enough and are not always large enough to live on.

While staff writers are paid a regular salary (though generally not a very high one), a freelancer gets paid only when he or she sells an article. Fees could range from as low as twenty dollars to two thousand dollars or more depending on the publication. But even with a high-paying magazine, writers often have to wait until the story is published before they are paid. Because publishers work so far ahead, planning issues six months or more in advance, payment could be delayed from three months to a year or more.

To the freelancer's advantage, sometimes the same article can be sold to more than one magazine or newspaper. These resales are an important way to increase earnings. And you can also earn additional money if you provide your own photographs to illustrate your articles.

What It's Really Like

As we have seen, there are many types of magazines to write for. Read the following account of a travel writer to get an overview of this career.

Carol Perry, Travel Writer

Carol Perry has been a travel writer for more than fifteen years. She also writes novels for middle school children as well as articles on ecology, historic houses, antiques, and collectibles. In addition to her traveling and writing, Carol enjoys teaching others how to write travel articles, and she frequently conducts seminars and classes.

The Role of the Travel Writer. The genre of travel writing includes several types of articles. A service article might help readers choose the best luggage or give tips on how to travel with pets.

A destination piece takes a general look at a city or country, providing information on how to get there and suggesting sights, restaurants, and hotels.

A third type of article focuses on a specific angle, such as the architecture or history of a district, a famous person who might have lived there, or an unusual local event.

A travel writer uses every opportunity to find something of interest to document. Even an event or a neighborhood close to home can provide material for an entertaining story.

How Carol Perry Got Started. Carol has always enjoyed traveling, and she keeps a detailed journal of her journeys. She also collects brochures and pamphlets that are available from chambers of commerce in all the destinations she visits. When she decided to begin writing, travel was the first topic that presented itself. Carol's first article was about side trips in London, and she still writes about side trips and day trips in different destinations.

Desirable Traits for a Travel Writer. Like all writers, travel writers must have a love of both their vocation and their subject. Carol says, "In addition to a love of travel, travel writers must also love the written word. They have to be skilled writers and must understand what elements make a story special or interesting."

Although college is not a prerequisite, Carol believes that it is beneficial as a way to learn the basics of writing. In addition, she recommends that writers improve their craft by attending seminars, lectures, and workshops and by reading what other writers write. For travel writers, it is sometimes also necessary to know how to take photographs to accompany the articles.

The Upsides of Travel Writing. For a writer who loves travel, the upsides of this career might seem obvious. Carol says, "I love to travel! I've seen the Parthenon in Greece lit up in a spectacular display at night. I've been on whale-watching assignments—you hear this whoosh and all of a sudden forty tons of whale comes roaring out of the water next to you and slams back down. Travel writing has allowed me to see and do things I never would have been able to do otherwise. And I've met wonderful people. When you say the magic words, 'I'm a writer,' it's amazing how lovely and helpful people are."

Advice from Carol Perry. Carol has some tips for aspiring travel writers. "Spend a lot of time composing your query letter," she advises. "That's what grabs an editor's attention. Make your article proposal sounds intriguing, interesting. Find your information from your own firsthand experiences or from the information the chamber of commerce or the library can provide. Take your own photographs or ask the tourist bureau to lend you some.

"And if someone has been helpful to you, giving you information for your story, make sure you send a thank-you note."

Writing Nonfiction Books

Writers of nonfiction have a distinct advantage over fiction writers. Each year, more than two nonfiction titles are published for every fiction book. This means that there are more than twice as many opportunities for the beginning nonfiction book writer to break in and get published. In fact, it's probably safe to say that any competent writer with a little market savvy can find a home for his or her writing.

But you might be thinking that a nonfiction writer needs to be experienced in a specialized field of knowledge before even thinking about writing a nonfiction book. After all, a fiction writer can rely on imagination; nonfiction writers have to be experts.

Right?

Wrong.

Nonfiction book writers do not have to start out as experts, though many of them end up that way by the time they've finished. In this chapter you will learn how to go about gathering the information you need to propose, write, and publish your nonfiction book.

Where to Start

As with any book, you must start with an idea, a topic that interests you and that you would like to learn more about. The topics nonfiction writers write about cover everything under the sun. Here is just a small sampling of general categories that publishers are interested in.

Autobiography	How-to
Biography	Investing and Making
Career/Finding a Job	Money
Child Care	New Age/Spiritual
Cooking	Parenting
Dieting	Relationships
Health/Fitness	Self-help/Psychology
History	Textbooks
Hobbies	Travel

At this writing, among the current top fifteen bestselling nonfiction books are five autobiographies or memoirs, one biography, five political books, one diet/health book, and three relationship books. Most of these books have been written by famous people, but that doesn't mean that an unknown, competent writer can't get a foot in the door.

What to Do with Your Idea

Once you've decided on a topic, check what's already been written on the subject. Your book won't be published if it only duplicates the information of a hundred other books. However, if your book provides additional or different information from what is currently available—in other words, if your book will fill a gap in the marketplace—then you have a shot at getting it published.

Go to the library and the bookstore to see what's already out there. Check booksellers' websites. Note the publishers of similar titles because they might be the ones who will be interested in your book, too. Once you have examined the competing books, you can decide if your idea is still a good one.

The Next Step

Before you write your proposal, which is your entry into a literary agency or a publishing house, you have to make sure you can collect the information you will need to write your book.

If you already are an expert in a particular area—a hobby or form of cooking, for example—then you have a head start. But you will still need factual information to complete your book. Most nonfiction writers use two sources for information: books, articles, and documents on the subject; and interviews with professionals or experts in the field.

If you are writing a biography of a famous person, for example, you can study other books written about that person's life, and you can track down and interview people who know that person. If you want to write about gardening, you interview gardeners. If you want to write about money matters, you interview investment counselors, and so on.

Query Letters and Book Proposals

After you've done your initial research—you have your idea, you know what the competition is, and you know how to gather the information you'll need to write the book—you are ready to compose a query letter. This is basically a miniproposal, telling an editor or agent about your book idea, why you think it should be published, who the readers will be, and why you should be the person to write this book. You end your letter by offering to send a full proposal and sample chapters.

The proposal is a longer version of your query letter. It should include a table of contents that shows you know how to organize and present the material for your book, along with one or two sample chapters.

If the editor or agent likes your proposal, you'll probably be asked to send the completed manuscript. Few first-time writers can land a book contract without a finished book, but it does happen that a good proposal can get you a sale.

Your proposal could also save you the time of writing a book that will never get published. You might learn from the editors or agents that there is no interest in your idea for a number of reasons. Here are some possibilities:

1. There are too many similar books on the same subject.
2. There aren't any current books on the subject, but that's because earlier ones did not sell well.
3. The audience for your book is too narrow—not enough people would be interested in it to make publishing it financially worthwhile.
4. Your book doesn't cover enough ground.
5. Your book covers too much ground.

If your idea is turned down, don't get discouraged. The feedback you get from agents and editors can give you ideas for revising your book, or it might even lead you to a new topic altogether.

Rewards for the Nonfiction Book Writer

If you do receive that exciting phone call or letter informing you your book has been accepted, you can expect to receive a book contract that will spell out all the terms. An advance for a nonfiction book could range from one thousand dollars to even a million dollars or more, depending on how big the publishing house is, how timely and important your book topic is, and how many books the publishers believe they'll be able to sell. First-time writers should expect to fall somewhere at the bottom of the scale.

You will also be paid royalties, a percentage of the price of each book that sells, once the royalties accumulated exceed the amount of your advance. But while you're waiting for your advance or first royalty check, it would be a good idea to get started on that next book. Few people can retire after one book; most writers have to write many in order to support themselves. But writing a complete book, then getting it published, no matter the amount you're paid, is an accomplishment to be proud of, a reward unto itself.

What It's Really Like

Perhaps the following accounts of two nonfiction writers will spark your interest. Read on to see whether this career is for you.

Jan Goldberg, Author and Freelance Writer

Jan Goldberg has a B.A. in education from Roosevelt University in Chicago. Her articles have seen print in more than two hundred publications, including *Complete Woman, Opportunity Magazine, Chicago Parent,* and publications from the Pioneer Press group. She is the author of several books published by McGraw-Hill, including: *Careers in Journalism, Opportunities in Horticulture Careers, Opportunities in Research and Development, Opportunities in Entertainment, Careers for Adventurous Types and Other Go-Getters,* and *On the Job: Real People Working in Communications.* She is also codeveloper of the On the Job series.

How Jan Goldberg Started Writing. Jan's interest in writing began during childhood. "Writing was always my first love," she says. "My grandfather was a bookbinder, so as a little girl my sister and brother and I would make trips to his workplace on weekends, which was a special treat. I was so enthralled by the excitement of it—with colored pages and scraps of paper and books that seemed to be piled up to the sky—and the smell of it. I can still remember it, and I know that I made up my mind then I would do something with books and writing."

Although Jan is a certified elementary school teacher and taught for several years, her interest in writing never waned. She started writing poetry and then moved on to book reviews. She considered educational writing and completed some projects for Scott Foresman and Addison Wesley. Jan was working on textbooks and activity workbooks and realized that she preferred writing to teaching.

Jan contacted an educational publisher that handled magazines, and she began to write for *Modern Health* and *Career World.* She next began writing books for VGM Career Horizons and also branched out into other publications.

Jan says, "I really enjoyed teaching, and it was a tough call for me, but I've established myself now, and I'll stay with the writing. It's a good combination, though: writing and teaching."

A Writer's Life. "I consider my job to be among the most interesting jobs you could find, especially since I write both articles and books in a variety of subject areas," Jan says. "I'm constantly researching new subjects and learning something new. I feel as if I'm an explorer venturing into new territory every time I approach a new topic.

"This week I also attended a writers' conference, so that means my next project will be to follow up on the contacts I made with several magazine editors there. I'll be putting together my resume and published clips of my articles as samples of my writing."

A typical day for Jan involves performing several activities. She writes, contacts her editors, does research, and makes telephone calls to gather information.

As a freelance writer, Jan must always look ahead. "Everything I do, I do with an eye to the future," she says. "What projects will I be working on three months from now, six months from now, even a year from now? So I'm always planning and always at different stages with different projects."

The Ups and Downs of Writing. "The good part of all of this is that I can call my own shots and make my own schedule," Jan says. "The bad part is the same, because in order to meet my obligations and do a good job, I really do have to put in a lot of time. Some days could be twelve-hour days, and others, depending on deadlines and how many projects I have going on, I might be able to take some time off. Because I work in a home office, I can work whenever I want—but of course, because the work is always there, I never quite get away from it.

"Also, as a freelancer, you're self-employed, basically running your own business. You have to send out bills, keep good records, have several filing systems, and of course you have to know how to market and sell yourself well. You're doing everything any small-business person would do.

"What I like the most is the anticipation of new projects, new ideas, being allowed to be creative and doing new things. But writing is hard work—which a lot of people don't realize—and sometimes it isn't a lot of fun.

"For me, though, the most difficult part is negotiating contracts and trying to collect money that's owed to me."

Advice from Jan Goldberg. Jan has some advice for anyone interested in nonfiction writing. "You need to have a lot of projects going on at one time if you're going to make a living being a book author or freelance writer," she says. "As a novice, you have to be patient or you'll never make it. It's a slow process getting established. You have to pay your dues as in any other profession. You have to be persistent, and it requires a lot of discipline. And you can't really expect too much too soon.

"I've never really figured out an hourly wage for myself, but writing in general is not a high-paying profession. If you want to really make tons of money, you'd probably want to choose another career. Before you think about quitting your day job, you need to be sure how much money you'll be able to make to support yourself."

Jim Haskins, Biographer

Jim Haskins is in the middle of a very distinguished career, with 101 published books to his credit, one of which is *The Cotton Club*, which inspired a successful movie. His interests range from biography and music to history and language. He is also a full professor in the English department of the University of Florida in Gainesville. Jim's latest books include *Separate but Not Equal: The Dream and the Struggle*, *Black Stars of Civil War Times*, and *Black Stars of the Harlem Renaissance*.

How Jim Haskins Started Writing. Jim describes the start of his career as rather unexceptional. "In a way, I just fell into it," he says. "I didn't grow up thinking I wanted to be a writer—it's something I just did. I found I have a knack for it. Nothing drew me to writing; there were no influences, no Fitzgeralds or Hemingways."

Jim's first book, *Diary of a Harlem Schoolteacher*, wasn't even intended as a book at all. Jim planned to teach elementary school for only a year and kept a diary for his own benefit. An acquaintance who worked in publishing read the diary and felt it had potential, and that's how it became a book.

Doing the Research. Since Jim writes a great deal of biographical material, much of his research involves interviewing people. Sometimes the subject of the book agrees to be interviewed, but that is not always the case. When this happens, Jim interviews others, such as family and friends, who can offer insight into the subject's life.

"The great mistake people make is thinking that if a person is a 'name' you're going to get the story of his life directly from him," Jim says. "But it doesn't always happen that way. For example, with Michael Jackson, I talked to his brothers. . . . For the book I wrote on Richard Pryor, I talked to his lawyer, who happens to be my lawyer as well. With Magic Johnson, I talked to his parents and people who knew him and went to college with him. Stevie Wonder was one of the agreeable ones—I got to talk to him."

Jim warns potential biographers to keep their work in perspective. "I never tried to write a definitive book about anybody's life. If I finish it in 1993, by 1995 there's a lot more I could add. Books are not newspapers or current affairs; they're out of date as soon as they come out."

A Writer's Schedule. Like all writers, Jim has worked out a method that suits him. "I write in hotels and on airplanes and everywhere else. I don't use computers; I can't think on them. I write in longhand on yellow legal pads, then I type up the manuscript on an old Royal manual. Then someone enters it into the computer for me.

"For me writing is a job and a craft. There's nothing particularly romantic about it. Some days I don't write at all. I have to do a lot of reading and research and absorb it all before I sit down and write. Some days I read, and some days I think about what I want to write, and then when it comes, it comes. I'll sit and do it. That could be two or three o'clock in the morning."

Jim talks about how he chooses his topics. He says, "I only write about people I'm interested in or subjects I want to learn more about, and when I'm researching one subject I'll come across some interesting information that will lead me to the next project. Scott Joplin led into *The Cotton Club*, *The Cotton Club* led into the next one, and so on. I have friends all over the country who send me newspaper clippings I might be interested in. I'm not just beginning the process; writing books is an ongoing process. I'm always working on something."

The Upsides of Writing. Jim enjoys his work and finds mostly positives in his career. "I like that I have the freedom to do it, the leisure. Reading and writing are luxuries of the leisure class. You can't be a writer unless you're a reader. And you can't be a reader unless you have the time. One hopes that eventually you'll earn enough money to support yourself, but starting out you have to have money. If not, the wolf is always at the door, but you're willing to risk its being there. It's always hand-to-mouth. That's why a lot of writers do a lot of other things besides write."

Online Opportunities

The rapid growth and widespread availability of the Internet has created numerous job opportunities for those who have knowledge to share but still prefer to do the majority of their work alone. Many schools and universities offer online courses. Some programs are available only through the Internet, not at regular schools. And some enterprising introverts have designed their own programs of instruction in various disciplines.

Online instructors have expertise in virtually any topic and offer courses on a part-time basis just as they would at a two- or four-year college or adult education facility.

What It's Really Like

Read the following account of an enterprising online instructor to see whether you might be interested in sharing your knowledge with others.

Stephen Morrill, Online Instructor

Stephen Morrill has been a full-time freelancer for twenty years. In that time, he has written more than one thousand articles for national and local magazines and newspapers. His work has appeared in *New York Times Magazine*, *Business Age*, *The Robb Report*, *Florida Business*, and *Southern Homes*, among other publications. Stephen has also worked as the local correspondent in his home area for the wire service Reuters News Agency, and his work has been used by newspapers and radio and television stations around the world.

Stephen started teaching nonfiction writing for America Online in 1988. Since then, he has run WritersCollege.com, an online service that offers more than sixty courses and is one of the largest online correspondence writing schools.

How Stephen Got Started. "I learned about the job on AOL through another AOL teacher who knew that I taught nonfiction writing at a local school and in seminars and that I had been a full-time freelancer for ten years. He asked me to come to AOL and teach there. I first became a subscriber to the service, then sent a proposal and lesson plan to the Online Campus coordinator via e-mail. He let me try a freebie course first. Then I started teaching and getting paid."

What Online Teaching Involves. Stephen describes two of the courses he taught for AOL: Freelance Nonfiction Magazine Articles and Freelance Nonfiction Writing Business. The first was intended to teach students how to write a research-based, standard nonfiction magazine article. He taught students how to do this and guided them word by word through writing a short sample article.

The second course, Freelance Nonfiction Writing Business, was intended to teach students how to market themselves and how to run the business of nonfiction writing on a freelance basis. While the course covered writing for magazines, books, and assorted brochures and newsletters, the primary focus was the magazine market.

Each course involved a two-hour weekly session for eight weeks. The classes consisted of three parts. Each week Stephen uploaded materials for the students to read before the next class. During the sessions, Stephen interacted live online with his students. As he describes it, "In class we interact as much as the medium allows: we have questions and answers, and we do an in-class exercise or two. Each week students also receive an assignment to carry out."

The Upsides. This is what Stephen had to say about his job: "The job is really a lot of fun. I teach it for three reasons. First, I get cash for it. Second, I simply love to talk (or write) about freelancing, and I'm a good teacher, too. And third, it gets me pumped up for my own writing, sort of like going to weekend conferences but with pay."

The Work Involved. In addition to his online interaction with students, Stephen also spent a good deal of time off-line, critiquing student manuscripts. He believes that this is part of his responsibility as a teacher. Stephen says, "I'm very determined to tell them all I know and to give them their money's worth. Students need a three-inch loose-leaf binder to hold the material from one course."

Stephen's ability to work quickly keeps his off-line time down. He says, "I can critique a fifteen-hundred-word manuscript in about twenty minutes. This comes, frankly, from having seen almost every question or problem before and so having an answer ready at hand and also from just being a fast typist. And I am not ashamed to say 'I don't know' sometimes. I do usually try to suggest some other place to look for the answer."

An online setting allows the instructor to give a wealth of information to students because they can download materials to read on their own time. The interactive nature of the courses even allows for some lively question-and-answer sessions.

Advice from Stephen Morrill. Stephen offers this advice for anyone considering teaching an online course: "Do it only if you already teach somewhere else or have some experience in teaching. Regard it as an adjunct to your real job; it's that other job that gives you the expertise to teach. Be extremely computer literate and comfortable with, and knowledgeable about, the online Internet and Web worlds. Take a class or two online to see what it's all about before you jump in."

For More Information

The following publications provide a wealth of advice on where and how to submit your work and how to survive as a freelance writer.

Bowling, Anne, and Michael Schween, eds. *Novel and Short Story Writer's Market.* Cincinnati: F&W Publications. Annual.
   This guide provides more than nineteen hundred entries of fiction publishing opportunities, including big publishing houses, small presses, consumer magazines, and literary and small-circulation magazines. The guide also offers advice and inspiration from top editors and authors.

Brogan, Kathryn, ed. *Guide to Literary Agents.* Cincinnati: F&W
Publications. Annual.

*In addition to its more than five hundred listings of fee-charging and
nonfee-charging agents and what they handle, this guide showcases
several articles of interest to writers.*

Brogan, Kathryn, and Robert Lee Brewer, eds. *Writer's Market.*
Cincinnati: F&W Publications. Annual.

*This guide lists book publishers, agents, magazines, and other
publications to which writers can sell their work. It also includes
several articles offering advice about various aspects of freelance
writing. Visit the website at www.writersmarket.com.*

Cool, Lisa Collier. *How to Write Irresistible Query Letters.*
Cincinnati: F&W Publications, 2002.

Larsen, Michael. *How to Write a Book Proposal.* Cincinnati: F&W
Publications, 2004.

Pope, Alice. *Children's Writer's and Illustrator's Market.*
Cincinnati: F&W Publications. Annual.

*This guide can help aspiring writers and artists make sure their
submissions end up on the right desk. It contains nearly seven
hundred markets, including children's book publishers, magazines,
scriptwriting markets, greeting card companies, and markets for
writing and artwork by children.*

Writer's Digest Magazine
F&W Publications
4700 East Galbraith Road
Cincinnati, OH 45236

*This monthly publication covers every aspect of the writing life, from
magazine queries and articles to poetry, fiction, and nonfiction.
Information is also available at www.writersdigest.com.*

CHAPTER THREE

Artists

As an artist, you probably hope to carve a niche for yourself in a job that allows you to use your talents. There are a lot of choices, however, and the aim of this chapter is to help you narrow them down and find the career path that best suits your education, interests, and skills.

Within the many job titles open to artists, there are two that allow you the most independence: studio artist and freelance commercial artist. Although artists also work in art education, galleries, or museums, those settings, by their very nature, preclude the opportunity of working alone. More information about careers in those settings can be found in the books named at the end of the chapter and from the professional associations listed in the Appendix.

Studio Artists

You have completed an art degree program and worked extensively on your own to fine-tune your artistic skills. Your goal has always been to support yourself as an artist or craftsperson, perhaps even to have your own studio, a place in which to create and sell your work. Whether it's pottery or painting, sewing or stained glass, you can make a name for yourself and work full-time in your chosen area—without necessarily starving in an artist's garret.

Having said that, few studio artists can move immediately into a career that provides adequate financial support. It takes time to build a reputation or a clientele, and during those "lean years," many artists seek out additional avenues that can assure a regular paycheck.

Although some artists might fall into a variety of moonlighting occupations—anything from food service to secretarial work—the vast majority choose to stay in related fields. Those with a teaching certification may teach art in elementary or secondary schools, while those with master's or doctoral degrees may teach in colleges or universities.

Some fine artists work in arts administration in city, state, or federal arts programs. Others may work as art critics, art consultants, or as directors or representatives in fine art galleries; give private art lessons; or serve as curators setting up art exhibits in museums. You will find talented artists working in a variety of settings, many of which are covered in this chapter.

For the serious studio artist, the main goal is to create a work of art that combines and allows for the need for self-expression and the need to make a living. It can be done.

Fine artists advance as their work circulates and as they establish a reputation for a particular style. The best artists continue to grow in ideas, and their work constantly evolves over time.

Visual Artists

Visual artists, which includes studio (or fine) artists and illustrators, use an almost limitless variety of methods and materials to communicate ideas, thoughts, and feelings. They use oil paint, watercolor, acrylic, pastel, magic marker, pencil, pen and ink, silk screen, plaster, clay, or any of a number of other media, including computers, to create abstract or realistic images of objects, people, nature, topography, or events.

Whether an artist creates abstract or realistic works depends not so much on the medium, but on the artist's purpose in creating a work of art. Fine artists often create art to satisfy their own need for self-expression, and they may display their work in museums, corporate collections, art galleries, and private homes. Some of their work may be done on request from clients, but not as exclusively as that of graphic artists. (See the section on graphic artists later in this chapter.)

Studio artists usually work independently, choosing whatever subject matter and medium suits them. Usually, they specialize in one or two forms of art.

- **Painters** generally work with two-dimensional art forms. Using techniques of shading, perspective, and color mixing, painters produce works that depict realistic scenes or abstractions that may evoke different moods and emotions, depending on the artists' goals.
- **Sculptors** design three-dimensional art works either by molding and joining materials such as clay, glass, wire, plastic, or metal, or by cutting and carving forms from plaster, wood, or stone. Some sculptors work with mixed media, combining materials such as concrete, metal, wood, plastic, or paper.
- **Potters** work with a variety of clay materials—from low-fire clays to high-fire stoneware or porcelain—and either hand build their artwork or create different forms using a potter's wheel. They follow existing glaze recipes or experiment with different chemicals to formulate their own.
- **Printmakers** create printed images from designs cut into wood, stone, or metal, or from computer-driven data. The designs may be engraved, as in the case of woodblocking; etched, as in the production of etchings; or derived from computers in the form of ink-jet or laser prints, among other techniques.
- **Stained-glass artists** work with glass, paints, leading, wood, and other materials to create functional as well as decorative artwork such as windows, skylights, or doors.

- **Photographers** use their cameras, lenses, film, and darkroom chemicals the way a painter uses paint and canvas. They capture realistic scenes of people, places, and events, or through the use of various techniques, both natural and contrived, they create photographs that elicit a variety of moods and emotions.

Training for Studio Artists

Although formal training is not strictly necessary for fine artists, it is very difficult to become skilled enough to make a living without some training. Many colleges and universities offer programs leading to the bachelor of fine arts (B.F.A.) and master in fine arts (M.F.A.) degrees. Course work usually includes core studio art subjects, such as drawing, painting, printmaking, and sculpture, as well as art history and general classes in English, social science, and natural science.

Independent schools of art and design also offer postsecondary studio training in the fine arts leading to an associate of arts or bachelor of fine arts degree. Typically, these programs focus more intensively on studio work than do the academic programs in a university setting. The National Association of Schools of Art and Design accredits more than two hundred postsecondary institutions with programs in art and design; most award a degree in art.

Formal educational programs in art also provide training in computer techniques. Computers are used widely in the visual arts, and knowledge and training in computer graphics and other visual display software are critical elements of many jobs in these fields.

Career Outlook for Studio Artists

Because the arts attract many talented people with creative ability, the number of aspiring artists continues to grow. Consequently, competition for both salaried jobs and freelance work in some areas is expected to be keen.

Fine artists mostly work on a freelance, or commission, basis and may find it difficult to earn a living solely by selling their artwork. Only the most successful fine artists receive major commissions for their work. Competition among artists for the privilege of being shown in galleries is expected to remain strong, and grants from sponsors such as private foundations, state and local arts councils, and the National Endowment for the Arts should remain competitive.

Nonetheless, studios, galleries, and individual clients are always on the lookout for artists who display outstanding talent, creativity, and style. Talented fine artists who have developed a mastery of artistic techniques and skills, including computer skills, will have the best prospects for success.

Working Conditions

Artists generally work in art and design studios located in commercial spaces or in their own home studios. Some artists prefer to work alone; others prefer the stimulation of having other artists nearby. For the latter group, sharing space with other artists is often a viable alternative to the lone studio—both for camaraderie and for economics. The trend in many large cities, and even in more out-of-the-way areas, is toward shared space in cooperatively owned studios or in rented space in converted warehouses or storefronts.

Artists generally require well-lighted and well-ventilated surroundings because some art forms create odors and dust from glues, paint, ink, clay, or other materials.

Although most fine artists are usually self-employed, working in their own studios, they still depend on stores, galleries, museums, and private collectors as outlets for their work. Others have what many consider to be the ideal situation—a working studio and storefront combined. Still others follow the art-fair circuit, packing up their work to tour the country on a regular basis, deriving most if not all of their income from this source alone.

However, many artists will tell you that any of the above options can be risky, with no guarantee of sales. The art-fair circuit, in particular, can be unreliable, vulnerable to the vagaries of the weather and the whims of impulse buyers or true art lovers and collectors.

Earnings

The gallery and artist predetermine how much each earns from a sale. The gallery keeps a percentage of the sale price, usually 40 to 50 percent of the total, with the artist receiving the remainder.

Earnings for self-employed artists vary widely. Some charge only a nominal fee while they gain experience and build a reputation for their work. Others, such as well-established freelance fine artists and illustrators, can earn more than salaried artists. Many, however, find it difficult to rely solely on income earned from selling paintings or other works of art. Like other self-employed workers, freelance artists must provide their own benefits.

Median annual earnings of salaried fine artists, including painters, sculptors, and illustrators, were $35,260 in 2002. The middle 50 percent earned between $23,970 and $48,040. The lowest 10 percent earned less than $16,900, and the highest 10 percent earned more than $73,560.

What It's Really Like

What better way to learn how to go about starting your career as a professional artist than to hear it from someone who found a way to make a success of it?

Jim Anderson, Stained-Glass Artist

Over the last twenty-five years, Jim Anderson has established himself as a successful stained-glass artist in Boston. His studio on Tremont Street in the revitalized South End neighborhood is called Anderson Glass Arts. Jim attended Boston Museum School of Fine Arts and Massachusetts College of Art and graduated with a B.F.A. and a teaching certificate.

His website, www.jimandersonstainedglass.com, describes him as "artist, craftsman, architect, and restorer." When did this well-known artist first begin to create? "I started drawing and painting when I was young," says Jim. "Even in my baby book it says stuff like 'Jimmy is creative,' 'Jimmy is artistic,' 'Jimmy can draw.' It's one of the areas where I got affirmation as a child.

"I found that I really loved the combination of art and architecture, as opposed to paintings that just hang on walls. I liked the fact that stained glass becomes a permanent part of a building—it becomes architectural art."

Jim's designs include many styles, traditional as well as contemporary. He creates hand-painted glass, like what is seen churches, and styles from different periods, such as Victorian, Federal, and Edwardian.

How Jim Anderson Got Started. After finishing at the Boston Museum School, Jim went to the Massachusetts College of Art to pursue a teaching certificate as a way to guarantee an income if he could not support himself as an artist. But during that time, Jim realized that he actually was supporting himself after all. He started making windows for people, and it paid his way through college.

Jim recalls being fascinated by church windows as a child, and at age twenty-six he designed his first, in St. George's Greek Orthodox Church in Hyannis. "Now I'm amazed at that kind of undertaking for such a young man," Jim says in retrospect. "I remember that my colleagues in New York and other places were astounded that the commission for a church was given to such a young artist."

Jim says, "Commissions started coming because people saw the work I did on my own house. I own a brownstone in the South End, which is the largest Victorian neighborhood in America with over two thousand structures intact, bowfronts and brownstones.

"I set up a workshop on the ground level of the town house so I'd have a place to work, then I did my doorways first. Other neighbors saw them and really loved them. Some of my neighbors were professional architects, and they asked if I'd do their doors. Then other people saw the work, and it mushroomed. Over the years, I've done ten or fifteen doors on my street alone, and then other people on different streets started seeing them and hiring me."

It wasn't long before the *Boston Globe* published an article about Jim's work. Other papers followed suit, and a television documentary about revitalizing an old art form included Jim's work as well. Soon Jim was getting even more work and moved his studio out of his home to a more visible commercial area.

He hired assistants to help him and to do repair and restoration work. The number of assistants at one time depended on the economy and how much work Jim had. He would hire assistants when he had enough work, but he had to let them go if things slowed down. Since Jim's reputation has spread, however, he has employed a fully trained staff in his studio.

The Upsides. Jim describes his love for his work: "I like going to people's houses and making beautiful windows they really love and that I feel are appropriate for their homes. I wouldn't put a modern window in a Victorian, for example, because it wouldn't be suitable.

"I meet a lot of interesting people in my work. Maybe it's because it's an unusual art form, and it's usually interesting people who want it.

"The work is fun and challenging, and I'm always learning something new. The older I get, the more complicated and sophisticated the commissions get."

The Financial Picture. Jim is honest about the finances of his profession. "Money doesn't come in regularly, but it always seems to come in," he says. "Sometimes in big chunks, sometimes in little chunks. I never know when or what, but I haven't starved, and I haven't not paid my bills yet."

Advice from Jim Anderson. His years as a professional artist allow Jim to offer some advice to those who hope to follow in his footsteps. "Follow your dream. Listen to your gut on what to do. Visualize what you want for yourself, then slowly go toward it.

"But start slowly," he warns. "In my first studio, I made work-tables out of plywood and other basic, simple things I could find. Nothing fancy or expensive—whatever I could scavenge. I've refined the space over time. Don't spend too much as you go along. Let your business build up and don't overextend yourself.

"There are cooperative buildings for artists in lots of major cities now. It's nice to work around other artists and share old warehouse space. It gives you a lot of exposure, plus it keeps you in the art community, and the rents are usually reasonable.

"Just work hard and keep an eye on every aspect of the business, including the bookkeeping."

Artisans

There are myriad art and craft forms, and a word should be said here about the prudence of combining the two in a chapter dedicated to artists. There are some who would debate whether "crafts" are true art; however, serious quilters, basket weavers, woodworkers, and all the other artisans who work with their hands to create pleasing and commercially accepted works of art face the same challenges in making a living as do fine painters or sculptors.

For those who prefer the stability of job security and a dependable income, there is another setting that should be considered where artists and artisans may create their art and be gainfully employed while they do so, either in a full- or part-time capacity. This is a living history museum.

Living History Museums

A living history museum is a vibrant, active village, town, or city where the day-to-day life of a particular time period has been authentically re-created. Once you step through the gates, you leave the present behind. The houses and public buildings are restored originals or thoroughly researched reproductions. Interiors are outfitted with period furniture, cookware, bed linens, and tablecloths. Peek under a bed and you might even find a two- or three-hundred-year-old mousetrap.

Colonial Williamsburg in Virginia and Plimoth Plantation in Massachusetts are just two examples of living history museums. Addresses of these and others can be found at the end of this chapter.

These large enterprises offer employment for professional and entry-level workers in a wide variety of categories. Positions that would be of particular interest to art majors are costumers and artisans in the historic trades.

Most living history museums employ skilled artisans to demonstrate early crafts and trades. Some of these artisans perform in the first-person, playing the role of a particular character of the time. Others wear twentieth-century clothing and discuss their craft from a modern perspective.

Residents in living history museums wear the clothing of the day and discuss their dreams and concerns with visitors as they go about their daily tasks. If you were to stop a costumed gentleman passing by and ask where the nearest McDonald's is, he wouldn't have any idea what you were talking about—unless he thought to direct you to a neighbor's farm. He might even do so using the dialect of his home country.

In the stores and workshops lining Duke of Gloucester and Francis Streets in Colonial Williamsburg, you will find harness makers, milliners, tailors, needleworkers, silversmiths, apothecaries, candle makers, bookbinders, printers, and wig makers.

In the Pilgrim Village and Crafts Center at Plimoth Plantation, coopers, blacksmiths, joiners (cabinetmakers), potters, basket makers, and weavers are re-creating items from the year 1627, seven years after the *Mayflower* landed at Plymouth Rock. Most of the items the Pilgrims used in 1627 were brought with them on the *Mayflower* or imported later. Because the Pilgrim Village at Plimoth Plantation is time specific to the year 1627, only those crafts that were practiced then are demonstrated. In addition to their principal occupation as farmers, pilgrims in 1627 were coopers, blacksmiths, thatchers, and house builders. The interpretive artisans perform in costume and play the role of designated pilgrims documented to have lived in Plymouth during that year.

In addition to doing demonstrations, artisans often produce many of the items used on display in the various exhibits. These items include the furniture, cookware, and sometimes even the actual buildings.

Job Strategies

The competition is fairly high for artisan or costumer positions at living history museums. For example, the wardrobe department at Plimoth Plantation is a small one, currently employing only four workers. Other larger living history museums, such as Colonial Williamsburg, need more people. A good way to get a foot in the door is to work as a volunteer or apply for an apprenticeship, internship, or work-study position. Many start out as character interpreters or presenters, then move into their chosen position when openings occur. Because of limited budgets and a low turnover rate, openings are rare.

Salaries for artisans within living history museums differ depending on whether they are full-time or part-time. The latter group earns an hourly wage ranging between $7.50 and $10. A new graduate just starting out full-time could expect to earn in the high teens to midtwenties, depending on the location and available funding.

What It's Really Like

Four artisans employed with Plimoth Plantation share their stories. Read on to see whether any of these careers might be of interest to you.

Tom Gerhardt, Cooper

Tom Gerhardt interprets the character of one of the most famous Pilgrims, John Alden. Alden was a cooper who worked both inside a one-room cottage he shared with his wife and two children and in the adjoining yard.

Tom makes barrels and other wooden containers, such as buckets and churns, while answering visitors' questions about life in seventeenth-century Plymouth. He says, "Although in Europe you could still find people practicing the craft as it once was done, there are only a few barrel makers in this country. Wooden barrels are made mostly for the wine and spirits industry, but now it's a mechanized craft using power tools and machinery. The finished product is the same as the old craft, but the method is different. We practice the craft as it was done in the 1600s, using only hand tools."

In addition to his duties as an interpretive cooper, Tom is also responsible for general woodworking. He is one of several pilgrims building a new house on the grounds.

"What I enjoy most about Plimoth Plantation is that there are a number of very creative and talented people here," Tom says. "If you're willing to do the work, you can learn a good deal for yourself, while at the same time you're educating the visitors.

"There are so many people who will help you—you can be inspired by what they're doing; and you have the time to explore and develop your skills."

Tom Gerhardt's Background. Tom's interest in history began as a child. His father was a volunteer in charge of a small museum in Virginia, and on vacations he took the family all over the country visiting other museums. It was on one of these trips Tom first discovered Plimoth Plantation.

Later, Tom took a few courses under a master cooper in Portsmouth, New Hampshire, and attended college for a couple of years, studying general liberal arts and theater. He worked in the technical end of theater for a while but decided he wanted a change. Since he'd always been interested in the re-creation of history, in 1985 he returned to Plimoth Plantation and applied for a job as an interpreter.

Deb Mason, Potter

Plimoth Plantation also operates the Crafts Center, where other seventeenth-century crafts are demonstrated. Potters, joiners, basket makers, weavers, and a gift shop share space in a converted carriage house. Artisans in the Crafts Center wear twentieth-century clothing and discuss their work from a modern viewpoint.

Four potters alternate shifts to demonstrate to visitors the art of seventeenth-century throwing techniques. They also make all the pieces that are used in Pilgrim Village by the interpreters. During the winter months when the museum is closed to visitors, the potters make enough items to replenish their stock.

In addition to her own home studio, where she teaches pottery classes, does commission work, and makes pieces for display at various galleries, Deb Mason spends two eight-hours days a week in the Crafts Center and is the supervisor of the other potters.

"In the Crafts Center we don't claim to be seventeenth-century people because pottery wasn't done in the village in 1627," Deb explains. "But because of this, we have an advantage. We can talk to visitors in a way that's totally different from the interpreters. A visitor might go to the village, then come back to the Crafts Center to ask a question that the seventeenth-century interpreters couldn't answer. The interpreters have to speak as though they are Pilgrims. They wouldn't have any knowledge beyond 1627."

The potters work with twentieth-century equipment, although they have discussed using a wood-burning stove and kick wheel, both implements of an earlier time. The electric wheels that they use make throwing pots appear faster and easier than it was in the seventeenth century, but the basic technique is the same.

Deb explains that some difficulty arises from the need to make only period pieces. "For example," she says, "we're trying to find the right clay bodies to work with. We have a few original pieces on display to study, and you can see the clay color and texture. We've been experimenting, trying to develop clay bodies that are close to the original.

"That's been fairly successful, but we're having a tough time with glazes. They used a lot of lead back then. In fact, most every glaze was lead based. Because we sell the pieces we make in the gift shop and they're also used in the village every day, we've been trying to get away from lead. It's hard to come up with glazes that have the same shine and the same colors; lead has a very typical look. We're using a ground glass that melts at a low temperature, which is a characteristic of lead, and it produces similar results."

The potters at the Crafts Center make a variety of period items, including ointment pots, apothecary jars, bowls, porringers, oil lamps, candlesticks, and pipkins (little cooking pots with a side handle and three legs). They also make three-handled cups, which are popular in the gift shop (Pilgrims often shared their eating and drinking implements, so three people could use one cup).

"Back then the pottery was hastily thrown," Deb explains. "There's a real earthy quality to the pieces. Their perception of what was beautiful and what was utilitarian was different. What they strove for was extremely rough by today's standards.

"My biggest problem is remembering not to throw too well. The advantage to that, though, for potters wanting to work here, is that a high degree of skill is not necessary."

Deb Mason's Background. Deb earned her B.A. in art with a major in ceramics in 1973 from Bennington College in Vermont. She taught ceramics full-time for thirteen years at a private school and was the head of the art department her last few years there. She joined the staff at Plimoth Plantation in 1992.

Patricia Baker, Costumer
Most living history museums employ professional costumers to keep their character interpreters and presenters outfitted in

authentic period clothing. Costumers generally work behind the scenes reproducing the apparel the average inhabitant would have worn.

Patricia is wardrobe and textiles manager at Plimoth Plantation. Her office and work space occupy a section of a converted dairy barn on the grounds of the museum. The atmosphere is that of a cozy living room with a lot of shelves and fabrics draped here and there, sewing machines and rocking chairs, a large cutting table, garment racks, and a radio.

"The clothes my department makes are common to what the middle class would have worn," she explains. "We provide our interpreters with enough clothing so they can dress authentically from the skin out. They don't even have to wear modern underwear if they don't want to."

Patricia explains that the basic undergarment for both men and women is a knee-length linen shift. The men dress in breeches and a doublet, which is a close-fitting jacket that falls just above the waist. The breeches are tied to the jacket with laces.

Women wear a plain corset over their shifts, giving them a smooth, cone-shaped look. Next come a number of petticoats and skirts and a padded roll to enhance the hips; waistlines are raised and meet in a point. The clothing is made of wool, linen, and cotton, all naturally dyed. The costumers' goal is to duplicate the materials used in the seventeenth century, as well as the construction techniques, such as sewing by hand.

The costumers also make all of the household furnishings used for display in the exhibits, such as sheets, pillow cases, feather and straw beds, paneled bed curtains, tablecloths, napkins, and cupboard cloths.

Maintenance and repair of existing costumes and furnishings are also part of the costumers' duties, as well as conducting research to keep the creations accurate for the particular time period. Since few articles have survived since the seventeenth century, the costumers must find other sources of information about the period. They use paintings, engravings, woodcuts, written descriptions, diaries, and plays to gather descriptions of the clothing and home furnishings of the period. They also study garments that are on display in other living history museums.

Patricia Baker's Background. Patricia graduated from the Massachusetts College of Art in 1976 with a bachelor of fine arts degree in crafts. Her concentration was in fabrics and fibers. She immediately began work at Plimoth Plantation as a character interpreter. In 1985 she joined the wardrobe department and became its head the following year.

Joel Pontz, Joiner

Joel Pontz supervises all interpretive artisans at Plimoth Plantation. He also serves as a character interpreter for the farmer John Adams and demonstrates his joinery skills in the Crafts Center.

Joel describes his job: "I step back and forth between the seventeenth and the twentieth centuries. Several days a week I'm in costume in the village as John Adams, picking my share of rutabagas or building small animal shelters or fences. On the other days I'm in modern clothing in the Crafts Center, demonstrating joinery."

Joiners were the principal furniture makers of the seventeenth century, before cabinetry became popular.

The joiners at the Crafts Center work before the public and behind the scenes. They make the furniture for Plimoth Plantation, including large cupboards, bedsteads, and chairs. They even make children's toys and mousetraps. They use various types of saws and hand tools, such as axes, planes, gimlets, and augers. The joiners do not use any power tools, since these would alter the texture and style of the finished product.

As Joel says, "We don't want to demonstrate any crafts in the village section of the museum that weren't practiced at the time. It would be anachronistic."

Joel advises taking a few courses in historic trades or historic preservation. "But," he cautions, "the skills we need are particular to Plimoth Plantation. Outside courses would be painted with such a broad brush, but what's done at Plimoth Plantation is very focused on a particular group of people in a very short time span.

"The best qualification would be a lot of hand-tool work. The tools haven't changed that much over the centuries. Try taking a tree and make a table or a chair from it. That's the best way to learn the art."

Joel Pontz's Background. Joel Pontz grew up near Plimoth Plantation and started working there as a volunteer Pilgrim after school and on weekends. In 1973 he became a full-time interpreter. He learned his joinery skill on-site from the other staff members and the research department.

"I hated woodworking in school," Joel admits. "It wasn't until I started working at the plantation using hand tools and trying to decipher how things were made that it became interesting for me. The historical aspect of it was what fascinated me. If it were just doing straight carpentry, I probably wouldn't have stayed with it."

Commercial Artists

Commercial artists, also known as graphic artists, and illustrators put their artistic skills and vision at the service of commercial clients, such as major corporations, retail stores, and advertising, design, or publishing firms. Their lot in life is much more secure than that of the studio artist, although a regular paycheck doesn't always guarantee the artistic freedom the former group enjoys.

Graphic artists, whether freelancers or employed by a firm, use a variety of print, electronic, and film media to create art that meets a client's needs. Graphic artists are increasingly using computers to produce their work instead of the traditional tools, such as pens, pencils, scissors, and color strips. Computers enable them to lay out and test various designs, formats, and colors before printing a final design.

The Role of the Graphic Artist

Graphic artists perform different jobs depending on their area of expertise and the needs of their employers. Some work for only one employer; other graphic artists freelance and work for a variety of clients.

- **Graphic designers** may create packaging and promotional displays for a new product, the visual design of an annual report and other corporate literature, or a distinctive logo for a product or business. They also help with the layout and design of magazines, newspapers, journals, and other publications and create graphic images for television.
- **Illustrators** paint or draw pictures for books, magazines, and other publications; films; and paper products, including greeting cards, calendars, wrapping paper, and stationery. Many do a variety of illustration formats, while others specialize in a particular style. Increasingly, illustrators work in digital format, preparing work directly on a computer.
- **Medical and scientific illustrators** combine drawing skills with knowledge of biology or other sciences. Medical illustrators draw illustrations of human anatomy and surgical procedures. Scientific illustrators draw illustrations of animal and plant life, atomic and molecular structures, and geologic and planetary formations. The illustrations are used in medical and scientific publications and in audio-visual presentations for teaching purposes. Medical illustrators also work for lawyers, producing exhibits for court cases.
- **Fashion artists** draw illustrations of women's, men's, and children's clothing and accessories for magazines, newspapers, and other media.

- **Storyboard artists** draw the plans for TV commercials. Storyboards present TV commercials in a series of scenes similar to a comic strip so an advertising client (the company paying for the advertising) can evaluate proposed commercials. Storyboards may also serve as guides to placement of actors and cameras and to other details during the production of commercials.

- **Cartoonists** draw political, advertising, social, and sports cartoons. Some cartoonists work with others who create the idea or story and write the captions. Most cartoonists, however, have humorous, critical, or dramatic talents in addition to drawing skills.

- **Multimedia artists** and **animators** work primarily in motion picture and video industries, advertising, and computer systems design. They draw by hand or use computers to create the large series of pictures that form the animated images or special effects seen in movies, television programs, and computer games.

- **Art directors** develop design concepts and review material that is to appear in periodicals, newspapers, and other printed or digital media. They decide how best to present the information visually so that it is eye-catching, appealing, and organized. Art directors decide which photographs or artwork to use and oversee the layout design and production of the printed material. They may direct workers engaged in artwork, layout design, and copywriting.

Working Conditions

Graphic artists work in art and design studios located in office buildings or their own homes. Those employed in publishing companies and design studios generally work a standard forty-hour week. During busy periods, they may work overtime to meet deadlines. Self-employed graphic artists can set their own hours, but they may spend much time and effort selling their services to potential customers or clients and establishing a reputation.

Possible Employers

Many graphic artists work part-time as freelancers while continuing to hold a full-time job until they get established. Others have enough talent, perseverance, and confidence in their ability to start out freelancing full-time immediately after they graduate from art school. Many do freelance work part-time while still in school in order to develop experience and a portfolio of published work before graduation.

The freelance artist develops a set of clients who regularly contract for work. Some successful freelancers are widely recognized for their skill in specialties such as children's book illustration or magazine illustration. These artists can earn high incomes and can pick and choose the type of work they do.

But more often than not, freelance careers take time to build. While making contacts and developing skills, many find work in various organizations.

Some commercial artists prefer full-time employment over freelancing. They find work in the following settings: advertising agencies, design firms, publishing companies, department stores, television production companies, motion picture companies, manufacturing firms, and the various agencies within the local, state, and federal government.

Training and Qualifications

Graphic Arts. Proven ability and appropriate training or other qualifications are needed for success in the graphic arts field. A portfolio showing evidence of appropriate talent and skill is an important factor used by art and design directors and others in deciding whether to hire or contract out work to an artist. The portfolio is a collection of handmade, computer-generated, or printed examples of the artist's best work. In theory, a person with a good portfolio but no training or experience could succeed in graphic arts. In reality, assembling a successful portfolio requires skills generally developed in a postsecondary art or design school program, such as a bachelor's degree program in fine art, graphic design, or visual communications.

Internships also provide excellent opportunities for artists and designers to develop and enhance their portfolios. Most programs in art and design also provide training in computer design techniques. This training is becoming increasingly important as a qualification for many jobs in commercial art.

Medical Illustration. The appropriate training and education for prospective medical illustrators is more specific. Medical illustrators must not only demonstrate artistic ability but also have a detailed knowledge of living organisms, surgical and medical procedures, and human and sometimes animal anatomy. A four-year bachelor's degree combining art and premedical courses is usually required, followed by a master's degree in medical illustration, a degree offered in only a few accredited schools in the United States.

Advancement Opportunities

In general, illustrators and designers advance as their work circulates and as they establish a reputation for a particular style. The best illustrators continue to grow in ideas, and their work constantly evolves over time.

Graphic artists may advance to assistant art director, art director, design director, and, in some companies, creative director of an art or design department. Some may gain enough skill to succeed as a freelancer or may prefer to specialize in a particular area. Others decide to open their own businesses.

Strategies for Job Hunting

As in any professional career, developing contacts and having a foot in the door at the type of organization for which you'd like to work are valuable assets. Internships are pathways to both. The best strategy is to plan ahead. During your undergraduate or graduate studies, arrange for as many internships as you can squeeze in—either full-time during the summers or part-time during semesters.

Learning how an advertising agency or a public relations firm or a TV studio functions will give you a broad overview and also help you build a successful portfolio. If an internship gave you a foot in the door, a professional and creative portfolio can open that door all the way. In addition, find yourself a mentor, someone who can critique your portfolio and advise you on how best to proceed.

Earnings

Median annual earnings of salaried art directors were $61,850 in 2002. The middle 50 percent earned between $44,740 and $85,010. The lowest 10 percent earned less than $32,410, and the highest 10 percent earned more than $115,570. Median annual earnings were $67,340 in advertising and related services.

Median annual earnings of salaried multimedia artists and animators were $43,980 in 2002. The middle 50 percent earned between $33,970 and $61,120. The lowest 10 percent earned less than $25,830, and the highest 10 percent earned more than $85,160. Median annual earnings were $58,840 in the motion picture and video industries.

What It's Really Like

Read on to learn firsthand about the work of a freelance illustrator to see whether this career might be of interest to you.

Peggy Peters, Freelance Illustrator

Peggy Peters teaches art at an alternative school in Texas; she also works as a freelance illustrator. Peggy has an undergraduate degree in fine arts, and she found the transition to commercial art difficult.

How Peggy Got Started. "I felt considerably handicapped trying to succeed in this profession," Peggy says. "Fortunately, I went for my master's at Syracuse University and earned my degree in illustration. The degree program was unique. It was through the independent studies department, and only working illustrators were accepted into the program. My group consisted of about sixteen people—illustrators from Alaska, Canada, California, England, Arizona, New York, Virginia, all over. I gained a broad overview of the profession, and the program was specifically geared to career development. I feel much more prepared now."

Peggy's first experience with commercial art was in junior high school, when she sold Beatles portraits. She worked as a set designer for public television and had her own studio for painting portraits and other commissioned works.

Several years ago she began to sell illustrations locally, working with fine arts organizations, theaters, and the opera company, among others. Peggy also produced all of the artwork for the 1997 World Flight project, in which pilot Linda Finch re-created the last flight of Amelia Earhart.

Peggy teaches full-time to keep health insurance and to pay off a student loan, so the amount of time she can devote to looking for commercial jobs is limited. She contacts local theater and fine arts organizations about using graphics for advertising. She is also learning computer graphics.

Advice from Peggy Peters. Peggy's experience gives her the insight to offer some good advice to aspiring graphic artists.

- Go to the best art school possible, such as Rhode Island School of Design, Chicago Art Institute, Syracuse University, or CalArts, among others.
- Learn computer graphics programs, such as PageMaker, Quark Xpress, Freehand, and Illustrator. Learn 3-D programs as well. It is advisable to do this before you go to college, if possible.

- Decide on the type of design or illustration you want to pursue and study the careers of artists working in that area. If possible, contact artists to learn about their careers.
- Be flexible. The field of commercial art changes rapidly, and you must be able to change with it.

Two of Peggy's most valuable tips are perhaps best stated in her own words: "Temperament is as important as talent. If you must make art to be happy, then you should pursue an arts career, but only if it is an absolute necessity. Being prolific is a great advantage also.

"The days of big advertising design firms are gone. More and more people are working freelance, and you don't have to be in New York City or Chicago to be successful anymore. With today's technology, illustrators are living and working everywhere these days."

. . . .

For More Information

The following books provide information on career paths available to artists:

Camenson, Blythe. *Great Jobs for Art Majors*, 2nd Edition. New York: McGraw-Hill, 2003.

Gordon, Barbara. *Opportunities in Commercial Art and Graphic Design Careers*, 2nd Edition. New York: McGraw-Hill, 2003.

For information about living history museums, contact:

Colonial Williamsburg
PO Box 1776
Williamsburg, VA 23187
www.history.org

Kootenai Brown Pioneer Village
1037 Beverley McLachlin Drive (Bridge Avenue)
Box 1226
Pincher Creek, AB T0K 1W0
Canada
http://telusplanet.net/public/kootenai

Nova Scotia Highland Village
4119 Highway 223
Iona, NS B2C 1A3
Canada
http://museum.gov.ns.ca

Old Sturbridge Village
One Old Sturbridge Village Road
Sturbridge, MA 01566
www.osv.org

Plimoth Plantation
PO Box 1620
Plymouth, MA 02362
www.plimoth.org

St. Augustine's Colonial Spanish Quarter
St. Augustine Trust for Historic Preservation (SATHP)
City of St. Augustine
PO Box 210
St. Augustine, FL 32085
www.historicstaugustine.com

CHAPTER FOUR

Researchers and Archivists

Research—in a wide variety of subject areas—is a major area of work that allows the freelancer independence. In this chapter you will learn about genealogy as a career option for freelance researchers and also be introduced to two researchers whose jobs don't fall into any of the expected categories.

In addition, you will read about the career of an archivist, a professional who is responsible for maintaining valuable records often used in research work.

Genealogists

The study of genealogy, tracing family histories, has grown dramatically in popularity in recent years. Almost everyone has a keen interest in his or her family background. Genealogists interview older family members; visit courthouses, cemeteries, and libraries; and spend hours poring through diaries, old newspaper accounts, marriage licenses, and birth and death certificates.

Many genealogy hobbyists take their interest one step further and become self-employed genealogists, helping others to dig up their family trees. Genealogists also are employed in historical societies and libraries with special genealogy rooms. The Church of Jesus Christ of Latter-day Saints in Salt Lake City, for example, maintains a huge repository of family information in its Family History Library. The library employs genealogists all over the world and provides a list of freelance researchers that includes genealogists who have been accredited through its own program. Contact information for the Family History Library is listed in the Appendix.

Other genealogists find work teaching their skills in adult education classes, editing genealogy magazines, or writing books or newspaper genealogy columns.

Most genealogists are not formally trained, though specializing in genealogy is possible through some university history and library science programs. Although there is not a specified curriculum for genealogists, the Board for Certification of Genealogists stresses the importance of certification for those interested in seriously pursuing this field.

Independent study courses are offered by the National Genealogical Society in Arlington, Virginia, and Brigham Young University in Provo, Utah. The National Institute on Genealogical Research in Washington, D.C., and Samford University Institute of Genealogy and Historical Research in Birmingham, Alabama, both offer intensive five-day programs covering various aspects of genealogy.

In addition, many local and state genealogy societies sponsor one- and two-day seminars. Information about these seminars is published in the newsletters of both the Federation of Genealogical Societies and the National Genealogical Society. These organizations also hold annual conferences at various sites nationwide. Information about useful publications and organizations is given at the end of this chapter.

Getting Started

One of the nice things about genealogy is that you can pursue it on your own before making a commitment to serious study. In this way, you can decide whether this is the right type of career for you. The National Genealogical Society suggests beginning with your own family tree as an introduction to genealogy and offers the following suggestions for how to get started:

- **Make a chart.** Begin with you, your parents, your grand-parents, and your great-grandparents. This will be the beginning of your family tree.
- **Search for records.** Look for birth, marriage, and death certificates and any other documents that might provide names, dates, and locations. Check your family's Bible records, old letters, and photographs for clues to people's identities and relationships. Label everything you find to make it easier to organize your research.
- **Talk to family members.** Encourage older relatives to talk about their childhoods and families and listen carefully for clues they might inadvertently drop. Learn good interviewing techniques so you ask questions that elicit the most productive answers. Use a tape recorder or camcorder and try to verify each fact through a separate source.
- **Visit the local library.** Become familiar with historical and genealogical publications and contact local historical societies. Check out the state library and the archives in your state capital. Seek out any specialty ethnic or religious libraries and visit cemeteries.
- **Visit courthouses.** Cultivate friendships with busy court clerks. Ask to see source records, such as wills, deeds, marriage books, and birth and death certificates that are not readily available from family members.
- **Enter into correspondence.** Write to other individuals or societies involved with the same families or regions. Contact foreign embassies in Washington, D.C. Restrict yourself to asking only one question in each letter you send. Include the information you have already uncovered, and include a self-addressed, stamped envelope as well as your e-mail address to encourage replies.
- **Use the Internet.** Many public records are available on the Internet. In addition, there are websites designed specifically for genealogical research. Some sites offer full access only to those who pay a registration fee; some offer software that

allows you to keep track of your research. Two popular sites are www.genealogy.com and www.ancestry.com.

- **Keep painstaking records.** Use printed family group sheets or pedigree charts. Develop a well-organized filing system so you'll be able to easily find your information. Enter your research information into a database if possible. Keep separate records for each family you research.
- **Contact the National Genealogical Society.** Browse the online bookstore for helpful publications. You can enroll in a home-study course titled American Genealogy: A Basic Course or take a course in the Online Learning Center. Contact information is listed in the Appendix.

Earnings for Genealogists

According to the Society of Professional Genealogists, most genealogical practices charge by the hour and also bill for out-of-pocket expenses, such as photocopies, telephone calls, travel, and vital-records fees. Hourly rates range from about $15 to $100, with the average falling between $25 and $60. Fees vary among professionals, depending upon experience, credentials, specialty, and geographic area. Highly skilled experts who specialize in unusually difficult research problems may charge higher rates.

What It's Really Like

Although not genealogists, the following two freelance researchers provide accounts of what it's like to be involved in other areas of research. Perhaps one of their stories will be of interest to you.

Valarie Neiman, Academic Researcher

Valarie Neiman formed EVN Flow Services in 1993. Through her home-based business she provides research and editing services and does academic, business, and creative writing. She earned her B.S. in business administration in 1980 from Arizona State

University in Tempe and her M.A. in human resources development in 1993 from Ottawa University in Phoenix.

"Research isn't what I do; it's part of who I am," Valarie says. "As one of the original latchkey kids in the 1950s, I spent a lot of time reading when I got home from school. To avoid being bored in class, I'd always read ahead in the textbooks.

"My first job fresh out of high school in 1966 was typing resumes. It's surprising how little they've changed in thirty years. The woman I worked for at the time began letting me write them, and soon I did the interviews as well."

How Valarie Got Started. Valarie held a variety of clerical and secretarial jobs and started college in her midtwenties. She later began studying for her master's degree while working for a defense contractor, but she lost the job and worked in several temporary positions. Her final temp assignment was researching and writing warehouse procedures. Valarie convinced the manager that it would be less expensive to hire her as an independent contractor rather than pay the temp agency. She also began soliciting work to help students with research projects.

"The rest, as they say, is history," says Valarie. "When I began EVN Flow (Ellwood and Valarie Neiman keep work flowing), my current business, I expected to help students format and type their papers. However, adult learners (over twenty-five) often haven't had training or don't remember how to write research papers. My work soon evolved into filling in the gaps in their abilities. Part of the job is reassuring them that they aren't stupid, letting them know I've developed a unique (and marketable) talent for pulling their work together into a package that makes them look good."

The Role of a Researcher. Valarie recognizes that most people think of researchers as scientists or academics. In her experience, however, research is part of nearly every job. She describes the goal of her projects as presenting knowledge and information in a different way, consolidating facts and assembling them to make a point, discovering new relationships in existing knowledge, or developing background and authenticity.

Through EVN Flow, Valarie also tutors adults in planning, researching, and writing academic papers. She reviews and edits master's research and graduation review projects and is under contract with Ottawa University to read and edit first drafts of master's candidates' theses.

In addition, she collaborates on research and writing a series of booklets on pricing, niche marketing, networking, outsourcing, tax tips, and how to start a home-based business (published by the Home-Based Business Association of Arizona).

The Upsides. Valarie enjoys the variety that her work makes possible. Her days are all different, and each projects sends her in a new direction. She also likes the part of the job that appeals to her introvert side. Valarie says, "Had I realized years ago that I am what is gently referred to as an 'individual contributor,' I may have found my niche sooner. I prefer to work alone, without supervision. I focus on the task at hand and am goal-oriented enough to get it done so I can move to the next project."

Working as a freelancer means that Valarie can manage her time as she wants. "My time is mine to spend as I wish," she says. "Since I like variety and 'big' projects, I find I work for an hour or so on one, then shift to another, and so forth.

"Some days, I catch up on phone calls or maintenance, but if I have paying clients, I stay focused on them. Some days I work fourteen hours (rare), others only three or four. I have a wonderful, understanding boss."

The Downsides. Of course, there is also a downside to any job. According to Valarie, "One of the things I like least about my work is that it isn't full-time and can be seasonal. I began writing a novel to fill those dreaded unbillable hours. Of course, the part-time nature of the work is also one of the things I like best! I'm sure that others in various types of research positions make a living. By my own choice, I make enough to pay business expenses and to pay myself a small stipend. Because I am a business, all travel, postage, supplies, and capital equipment associated with my writing are considered tax-deductible expenses."

Advice from Valarie Neiman. Valarie offers some very specific advice for anyone considering a career as a freelance researcher. Here are her pointers for success:

- Read, read, read, research, research, research. Go to the library, get online, practice finding things. Interview people, create questionnaires, read magazines.
- Have a desire for knowledge. Be persistent, empathetic, and intuitive. Practice good judgment.
- Get a good education, up to a Ph.D. or postdoctoral work. The major doesn't matter as much as your ability to thrive in an academic environment where research is important.
- Gain as much varied experience as possible. Work in a variety of settings, such as government, corporations, and small businesses.
- Write an excellent resume and learn how to network to find jobs.
- Keep your writing skills sharp, since research alone is useless without the ability to present the results.
- Maintain the highest degree of ethical and honest behavior; respect clients' confidentiality.

Susan Broadwater-Chen, Information Specialist and Freelance Writer

Susan Broadwater-Chen owns Moonstone Research and Publications, her home-based business in Charlottesville, Virginia. She has a B.A. in humanities from Asbury College in Wilmore, Kentucky, and an M.A. in theological studies from Emory University in Atlanta, Georgia.

"I have an insatiable curiosity about just about everything, and I love to write," she explains. "I especially like the challenge of having to find something and the excitement that comes when I find it. I love libraries, books, and puzzles, and some of the searches that I do are very much like putting puzzles together."

How Susan Got Started. While attending Mountain Empire Community College in Virginia, Susan took as many computer courses as possible. She got a job at the University of Virginia as a program support technician, where part of her job included working with research assistants and editing.

Susan worked at the University for ten years, during which she took courses about the Internet and developing Web pages. She also ran a business from her home, doing research and editing for clients.

In 1986 Susan began her business on a part-time, moonlighting basis, and she has been working at it full-time since 1995. Once she had built up enough contacts and customers to become independent, she quit her job at the university and started publishing a monthly newsletter and running a Web page. When she realized that she could support herself by using her skills to expand her client base, Susan decided to devote herself full-time to the business.

The Job Description. Susan publishes a monthly newsletter for writers that focuses on Internet materials and resources. She also handles individual projects in which she assists authors in locating hard-to-find research.

Susan works with online author colonies to develop content for research libraries. This work involves researching antiquarian books, microfilm, and other resources to provide primary source materials and bibliographical information. Her company's website offers a page where writers or anyone else can download materials, some for free and others at a cost. She offers a clipping service for subscribers and holds a weekly online workshop to assist people with any questions they might have about finding research materials.

Running her own business means that Susan works very hard to be successful. Most of her customers need the information they are seeking in a hurry. Writing a monthly newsletter and submitting articles to online magazines is also time-consuming.

Susan's work day starts at 6:00 A.M. when she checks her e-mail and news services to see what will require her attention. After getting her son to the school bus, she prints articles to read and files them in topical folders. Susan stresses the importance of being organized to avoid becoming deluged with paper and unable to find what she needs. Next Susan works on the projects that she plans to sell. This part of her day involves reading and writing articles or finding out-of-copyright primary source material that she can edit and reprint for sale.

Her next task involves working on the content she is developing for the online services. She checks e-mail again and works on the requests that she received overnight. At this point, Susan takes a walk to refresh herself and have some time away from her desk.

When she returns to work, Susan writes at least one review or article for her newsletter. She explores potential Internet sources that she might consider reviewing, which involves taking notes and printing material to use the next day when she writes the article. She also logs into library card catalogs looking for materials that she might want to request through interlibrary loan.

The Upsides. "I like it when I can help people," Susan says. "It makes me feel good to know that they're happy with what I've found. When I've helped a person who is publishing a book and he or she sends me a copy of the book, I get personal satisfaction knowing that I've helped with the research that the book required. I also like the feeling I get when I find some really obscure fact and pull the needle out of the haystack."

The Downsides. "The downside is that sometimes I can't help people because the facts won't bear out what they want to write about." In addition, Susan's work schedule is very demanding. "Because I work at home, it's a relaxed atmosphere, but sometimes I feel really pressured because there seems to be so much to do and only a limited number of hours in a day.

"I usually work about eighty hours a week, which is forty more than when I worked for someone else. I have one morning that I spend in the library every week. The job is not boring, but it's not easy money either."

Advice from Susan Broadwater-Chen. Susan offers some sound advice about developing a research business:

- Learn everything possible about electronic databases and the Internet. Develop good library research skills and learn how to conduct interviews.
- Cultivate as many skills as possible and know where to look for specific material.
- Establish a client base and connections before attempting a full-time business.
- Submit articles to online publications and network with people who might need your services.

Archivists

Archives hold firsthand information, so they are valuable to anyone with an interest in the people, places, and events of the past. Genealogists, researchers, scholars, students, writers, and historians are among the vast number of people whose work can be enhanced by using archives.

The exact number is not known, but it's estimated that there are thousands of archives in North America. Over five thousand archives exist in the United States—each of the fifty states maintains a government archive, as do most city and county governments. The same types of archives are kept in Canada. Archives are also found in universities, historical societies, museums, libraries, and private businesses.

On the national level, the National Archives in Washington, D.C., looks after the records of the federal government. The Library of Congress provides information services to the U.S. Congress and technical services to all of the libraries across the country.

Library and Archives Canada, the federal archive of Canada, combines the services of the former National Library and the National Archive.

What Are Archives?

Although archives are similar to libraries, there are distinct differences between the two. Libraries typically house materials that are published and were created with the express purpose of broad dissemination. Archives typically hold materials that were created in the course of some business or activity but were never intended originally for public use.

For example, an archive might include letters from a Civil War soldier to his family. He wrote about his experiences and feelings and to let his loved ones know that he was still alive, surviving battle. He never would have imagined that his correspondence would one day appear in an archive. Inclusion in an archive gives his letters credibility and integrity as a historical source.

Archives handle collections that chart the course of daily life for individuals and businesses. Some archives specifically look after materials created by their own institutions. Coca-Cola Company, for example, set up an archive years ago to maintain a history of what the business did and how it prospered. New companies set up archives to keep documented records of their businesses.

Educational institutions such as universities or museums create archives that relate to their special research interests.

The material found in an archive can include letters, personal papers, and organizational records. Archives created within the last hundred years or so can also contain visual records, such as photographs, postcards, prints, drawings, and sketches. Today archives also collect phonograph records, audiotapes, videotapes, movie films, and computer-stored information.

The Role of an Archivist

As with libraries and archives, there are distinct differences between librarians and archivists, including the way they operate and the methods and techniques they use to handle material.

The greatest difference is that librarians look at materials they get on an item-by-item basis. Each book is a distinct entity evaluated separately from the other books. In an archive, on the other hand, a single letter would usually be part of a larger collection of letters. Archivists are interested in these as a group because one letter would only be a fragment. To really understand something about the past, the information needs to be synthesized and put together in a collection.

When archivists talk about their work, they discuss certain basic functions that are common to all archives. The numbers following the five areas below designate the percentage of time usually spent with each duty.

Arrangement and description of collections	60
Identification and acquisition of materials	10
Preservation of collections	10
Reference services	15
Community outreach and public affairs	5

The information that archivists collect, organize, and exercise control over takes many forms. Working in accordance with accepted standards and practices, archivists maintain these records to ensure their long-term preservation and easy retrieval by researchers.

Original records maintained by archivists can take many forms, such as photographs, films, video and sound recordings, computer tapes, and video and optical disks, as well as more traditional paper records, letters, and documents.

They also may be copied onto some other format to protect the original and to make them more accessible to the researchers who use the records. As various storage media evolve, archivists must keep abreast of technological advances in electronic information storage.

Archivists often specialize in an area of history or technology so they can more accurately determine what records in that area qualify for retention and should become part of the archives. They may also work with specialized forms of records, such as manuscripts, electronic records, photographs, cartographic records, motion pictures, or sound recordings.

Computers are increasingly being used to generate and maintain archival records. Professional standards for the use of computers in handling archival records are still evolving. However, computers are expected to transform many aspects of archival collections as computer capabilities and the use of multimedia and the Internet expand and allow more records to be stored and exhibited electronically.

Working Conditions

The working conditions of archivists vary. While some spend most of their time working with the public, providing reference assistance and educational services, many others perform research or process records, which often means working alone or in offices with only a few people.

Qualifications and Training

People get into the archives profession in a variety of traditional and unusual ways. Often in a small town, an archive is a closet in the back room of a local historical society's office. Someone volunteers to put it all together, thus becoming the keeper of the community's history, or its archivist.

In more traditional settings, employment as an archivist usually requires graduate education and related work experience. While completing their formal education, many archivists and curators work in archives or museums to gain the hands-on experience that many employers seek.

Although several undergraduate degrees are acceptable, a graduate degree in history or library science, with courses in archival science, is preferred by most employers. Some positions may require knowledge of the discipline related to the collection, such as business or medicine.

There are approximately sixty-five colleges and universities that offer courses or practical training in archival science as part of history, library science, or another discipline. At this time, there are no schools in the United States that offer a distinct master of archival studies degree. There are schools in Canada that offer the degree, which has been established according to guidelines set by the Association of Canadian Archivists.

Certification

The Academy of Certified Archivists offers voluntary certification for archivists. The designation Certified Archivist is obtained by those with at least a master's degree and a year of appropriate archival experience. The certification process requires candidates to pass a written examination, and they must renew their certification periodically.

Desirable Traits and Skills

Archivists need research and analytical ability to understand the content of documents and the context in which they were created and to decipher deteriorated or poor-quality printed matter, handwritten manuscripts, or photographs and films. A background in preservation management is often required of archivists because they are responsible for taking proper care of their records.

Archivists also must be able to organize large amounts of information and write clear instructions for its retrieval and use. In addition, computer skills and the ability to work with electronic records and databases are becoming increasingly important.

Getting Ahead

Many archives, including one-person operations, are very small and have limited opportunities for promotion. Archivists typically advance by transferring to a larger unit with supervisory positions. A doctorate in history, library science, or a related field may be needed for some advanced positions, such as director of a state archive.

Employment of Archivists

Archivists, along with curators and museum technicians, held about twenty-two thousand jobs in 2002. About 35 percent were employed in museums, historical sites, and similar institutions, and 15 percent worked for state and private educational institutions, mainly college and university libraries. Nearly 40 percent worked in federal, state, and local government.

Most federal archivists work for the National Archives and Records Administration; others manage military archives in the U.S. Department of Defense. Most federal government archivists work at the Smithsonian Institution, in the military museums of the Department of Defense, and in archaeological and other museums as well as historic sites managed by the U.S. Department of the Interior. All state governments have archival or historical-records sections employing archivists. State and local governments also have numerous historical museums, parks, libraries, and zoos employing curators.

Some large corporations that have archives or record centers employ archivists to manage the growing volume of records created or maintained as required by law or as necessary for the firms' operations. Religious and fraternal organizations, professional associations, conservation organizations, major private collectors, and research firms also employ archivists.

Job Outlook for Archivists

Competition for jobs as archivists is expected to be strong because qualified applicants outnumber job openings. The best opportunities should be for graduates with highly specialized training, such as master's degrees in both library science and history, with a concentration in archives or records management and extensive computer skills.

Employment of archivists is expected to increase about as fast as the average for all occupations through 2012. Jobs are expected to grow as public and private organizations emphasize establishing archives and organizing records and information and as public interest in science, art, history, and technology increases.

Museum and zoo attendance has been growing and is expected to continue to increase; however, museums and other cultural institutions can be subject to cuts in funding during recessions or periods of budget tightening, reducing demand for archivists.

Although the rate of turnover among archivists is relatively low, the need to replace workers who leave the occupation or stop working will create some additional job openings.

Earnings

Median annual earnings of archivists, as they are grouped with curators and museum technicians, were $35,270 in 2002. The middle 50 percent earned between $26,400 and $48,460. The lowest 10 percent earned less than $20,010, and the highest 10 percent earned more than $66,050.

Earnings of archivists vary considerably by type and size of employer and often by specialty. Median annual earnings of archivists in 2002 were $33,720 in museums, historical sites, and similar institutions. The average annual salary for archivists in the federal government in nonsupervisory, supervisory, and managerial positions was $69,706 in 2003; for museum curators, $70,100; museum specialists and technicians, $48,414; and for archives technicians, $37,067.

· ·

What It's Really Like

Read the following account of a professional archivist to see whether this career might be right for you.

John Fleckner, Archivist

John Fleckner is the chief archivist at the Smithsonian Institution's National Museum of American History. He arrived at the Smithsonian in 1982 with more than a decade's experience working as an archivist for the State Historical Society of Wisconsin. He is a past president of the Society of American Archivists and has acted as a consultant on many important archives projects, including the United Negro College Fund and projects exploring the history and archives of Vietnamese Americans and Native Americans.

How John Got Started. John did his undergraduate work at Colgate University in Hamilton, New York, earning a B.A. with honors in history in 1963. He earned his master's degree in American history at the University of Wisconsin in 1965.

John's initial interest was not in a career as an archivist. His original plan was to teach college-level history, until a university career counselor pointed him toward a graduate program in archives administration. At the time this seemed like a more profitable career choice, and John decided to pursue it.

Once he began doing archival work, John realized how much he enjoyed it. As he says, "I loved the intense, intimate contact with the 'stuff' of history. Before I completed my internship, I knew I wanted to be an archivist." During his own research as a graduate student, archived material had seemed antiseptic and lifeless to

John. Once he became an archivist, though, he found the materials thrilling and loved "the mystery, the possibilities of the records themselves."

The Role of the Archivist. The archive John is responsible for acquires collections from the outside and does not handle the records generated by the museum. The collections cover a wide range of subjects and are particularly strong in the areas of American music, advertising, and the history of technology.

At the Smithsonian, John oversees a professional staff of twelve archivists, three student interns, and close to twenty volunteers.

As an archivist, John makes decisions that will determine how future researchers access the records. In a sense, he gets to reconstruct the past and to imagine the future through the records he handles. John follows established techniques and methods and maintains standards against which his work is judged.

For More Information

There are several guides available for the aspiring genealogist. The following volumes are recommended by the Board for Certification of Genealogists:

Baxter, Angus. *In Search of Your Canadian Roots: Tracing Your Family Tree in Canada*. Baltimore: Genealogical Publishing Co., 2000.

Board for Certification of Genealogists. *The BCG Genealogical Standards Manual*. Orem, Utah: Ancestry, 2001.

Eales, Anne Bruner, and Robert M. Kvasnicka, eds. *Guide to Genealogical Research in the National Archives of the United States*, 3rd edition. Washington, D.C.: National Archives and Records Administration, 2000.

Greenwood, Val D. *The Researcher's Guide to American Genealogy*, 3rd edition. Baltimore: Genealogical Publishing Co., 2002.

Mills, Elizabeth Shown, ed. *Professional Genealogy: A Manual for Researchers, Writers, Editors, Lecturers, and Librarians.* Baltimore: Genealogical Publishing Co., 2001.

The following sources provide information about research methods and practices:

Booth, Wayne C., Joseph M. Williams, and Gregory G. Colomb. *The Craft of Research*, 2nd edition. Chicago: University of Chicago Press, 2003.

Lester, James D. *Writing Research Papers: A Complete Guide*, 11th edition. Lebanon, IN: Pearson Longman, 2004.

Ruszkiewicz, John J., Janice R. Walker, and Michael A. Pemberton. *Bookmarks: A Guide to Research and Writing*, 2nd edition. Lebanon, IN: Pearson Longman, 2002.

CHAPTER FIVE

Computer Professionals

M ost computer professionals spend a major portion of their time working alone. Although many projects start off as a group effort utilizing a team approach, in the end, the actual work gets done solo. In this chapter we will look at four computer careers and hear from a professional who works in the field. Read on to see whether this growing industry is where you'd like to be.

Career Opportunities for Computer Professionals

Systems analysts, computer scientists, database administrators, and computer programmers are major elements of the ever-expanding computer industry.

Systems Analysts

The rapid spread of computers and computer-based technologies has generated a need for skilled, highly trained workers to design and develop hardware and software systems and to determine how to incorporate these advances into new and existing systems. Although many narrow specializations have developed and no uniform job titles exist, these professionals are widely referred to as computer scientists and systems analysts.

Systems analysts solve computer problems and apply computer technology to meet the individual needs of an organization. They help the organization to realize the maximum benefit from its investment in equipment, personnel, and business processes. The responsibilities of systems analysts may include planning and developing new computer systems or devising ways to apply existing systems' resources to additional operations. They may design new systems, including both hardware and software, or add a new software application to harness more of the computer's power.

Most systems analysts work with specific types of systems that vary depending on the kind of organization they work for, such as business, accounting, financial, scientific, or engineering systems.

Systems analysts begin an assignment by discussing the system's problem with managers and users to determine its exact nature. Defining the goals of the system and dividing the solutions into individual steps and separate procedures, analysts use techniques such as structured analysis, data modeling, information engineering, mathematical model building, sampling, and cost accounting to plan the system. They specify the inputs to be accessed by the system, design the processing steps, and format the output to meet users' needs. They also may prepare cost-benefit and return-on-investment analyses to help management decide whether implementing the proposed technology will be financially feasible.

When a system is accepted, systems analysts determine what computer hardware and software will be needed to set the system up. They coordinate tests and observe the initial use of the system to ensure that it performs as planned. They prepare specifications, flow charts, and process diagrams for computer programmers to follow, then they work with programmers to debug, or eliminate errors from, the system.

One obstacle associated with expanding computer use is the need for different computer systems to communicate with each other. Because of the importance of maintaining up-to-date information, such as accounting records, sales figures, or budget projections, systems analysts work on making the computer systems within an organization, or among organizations, compatible so that information can be shared among them.

Many systems analysts are involved with networking, which means connecting all the computers internally (whether in an individual office, department, or establishment) or externally, because many organizations now rely on e-mail and the Internet. A primary goal of networking is to allow users to retrieve data from a mainframe computer or a server and use it on their desktop computers. Systems analysts must design the hardware and software to allow the free exchange of data, custom applications, and the computer power to process it all. For example, analysts are called upon to ensure the compatibility of computing systems between and among businesses to facilitate electronic commerce.

Computer Scientists

Computer scientists work as theorists, researchers, or inventors. Their jobs are distinguished by the higher level of theoretical expertise and innovation they apply to complex problems and the creation or application of new technology.

Those employed by academic institutions work in areas ranging from complexity theory to hardware to programming-language design. Some work on multidisciplinary projects, such as developing and advancing uses of virtual reality, extending human-computer interaction, or designing robots.

Computer scientists in private industry work in areas such as applying theory, developing specialized languages or information technologies, or designing programming tools, knowledge-based systems, or even computer games.

Database Administrators

With the Internet and electronic business generating large volumes of data, there is a growing need to be able to store, manage, and extract data effectively. Database administrators work with database management systems software and determine ways to organize and store data. They identify user requirements, set up computer databases, and test and coordinate modifications to the systems.

An organization's database administrator ensures the performance of the system, understands the platform on which the database runs, and adds new users to the system as needed. Because they also may design and implement system security, database administrators often plan and coordinate security measures. With the volume of sensitive data generated every second growing rapidly, data integrity, backup systems, and database security have become increasingly important aspects of the job of database administrators.

Computer Programmers

Computer programmers are the professionals who write, test, and maintain the detailed programs that computers must follow to perform their functions. They also conceive, design, and test logical structures for solving problems by computer. Many technical innovations in programming, such as advanced computing technologies and sophisticated new languages and programming tools, have redefined the role of a programmer and elevated much of the programming work done today.

Computer programs tell the computer what to do—which information to identify and access, how to process it, and what equipment to use. Programs vary widely depending upon the type of information to be accessed or generated. For example, the instructions involved in updating financial records are very different from those required to duplicate conditions on board an aircraft for pilots training in a flight simulator.

Although simple programs can be written in a few hours, programs that use complex mathematical formulas, whose solutions can only be approximated, or that draw data from many existing systems may require more than a year of work. In most cases, several programmers work together as a team under a senior programmer's supervision.

The specifications for programs are generally determined by software engineers and systems analysts. Computer programmers must convert the specifications into a logical series of instructions that the computer can follow. The programmer then codes these instructions in a conventional programming language, such as COBOL; an artificial intelligence language, such as Prolog; or one of the most advanced object-oriented languages, such as Java, C++, or Smalltalk. Programmers generally know more than one programming language and, because many languages are similar, they often can learn new languages relatively easily.

Many programmers update, repair, modify, and expand existing programs. They often use computer-assisted software engineering (CASE) tools to automate much of the coding process. Programmers also utilize libraries of prewritten code, which can then be modified or customized for specific applications. This also yields more reliable and consistent programs and increases programmers' productivity by eliminating some routine steps.

Programmers test a program by running it to ensure that the instructions are correct and that the program produces the desired outcome. If errors do occur, the programmer must make appropriate changes and check the program until it produces the correct results. This process is called testing and debugging. Programmers may continue to fix these problems throughout the life of a program. In a mainframe environment, which involves a large centralized computer, programmers may prepare instructions for a computer operator who will run the program.

Programmers often are grouped into two broad categories—applications programmers and systems programmers. Applications programmers write programs to handle a specific job, such as a program to track inventory within an organization. They may also revise existing packaged software or customize generic applications called middleware.

Systems programmers, on the other hand, write programs to maintain and control computer systems software, such as operating systems, networked systems, and database systems. Because of their knowledge of the entire computer system, systems programmers often help applications programmers to determine the source of problems that may occur with their programs.

Programmers in software development companies may work directly with experts from various fields to create software ranging from games and educational software to programs for desktop publishing and financial planning. Much of this programming takes place in the preparation of packaged software, which constitutes one of the most rapidly growing segments of the computer services industry.

Advanced programming languages and new object-oriented programming capabilities are increasing the efficiency and productivity of both programmers and users. The transition from a mainframe environment to one that is based primarily on personal computers (PCs) has blurred the once rigid distinction between the programmer and the user. Increasingly, adept end-users are taking over many of the tasks previously performed by programmers. For example, the growing use of packaged software, such as spreadsheet and database management software packages, allows users to write simple programs to access data and perform calculations.

Programmer-Analysts. In some organizations, particularly in small ones, programmer-analysts are responsible for both the systems analysis and the actual programming work. Programmer-analysts design and update the software that runs the computer. Because they are responsible for both programming and systems analysis, these workers must be proficient in both areas. As this dual proficiency becomes more commonplace, these analysts increasingly work with databases, object-oriented programming languages, client-server applications development, and multimedia and Internet technology.

Working Conditions

Computer systems analysts, database administrators, computer programmers, and computer scientists normally work in offices or laboratories in comfortable surroundings. They usually work about forty hours a week; however, evening or weekend work may be necessary to meet deadlines or fix critical problems that occur during off hours. As computer networks expand, more programmers are able to make corrections or fix problems remotely by using modems, e-mail, and the Internet to connect to a customer's computer.

Given the technology available today, telecommuting is common for computer professionals. As networks expand, more work can be done from remote locations through modems, laptops, e-mail, and the Internet.

Like other workers who spend long periods in front of a computer terminal typing on a keyboard, computer professionals are susceptible to eyestrain, back discomfort, and hand and wrist problems such as carpal tunnel syndrome or cumulative trauma disorder.

Qualifications and Training

Systems Analysts, Computer Scientists, and Database Administrators

There is no universally accepted way to prepare for a job as a systems analyst, computer scientist, or database administrator; however, most employers place a premium on some formal college education. A bachelor's degree is a prerequisite for many jobs, although some jobs may require only a two-year degree. Relevant work experience is also very important. For more technically complex jobs, applicants with graduate degrees are preferred.

For systems analyst, programmer-analyst, and database administrator positions, many employers seek applicants who have a bachelor's degree in computer science, information science, or management information systems (MIS). MIS programs usually are part of the business school or college and differ considerably from computer science programs, emphasizing business and management-oriented course work and business computing courses.

Employers are increasingly seeking individuals with a master's degree in business administration (M.B.A.) and a concentration in information systems as more firms move their businesses to the Internet. For some network systems and data communication analysts, such as webmasters, an associate's degree or certificate is sufficient. More advanced positions might require a computer-related bachelor's degree. For computer and information scientists, a doctoral degree generally is required due to the highly technical nature of their work.

Despite employers' preference for those with technical degrees, people with degrees in a variety of majors find employment in these occupations. The level of education and type of training that employers require depend on their needs. One factor affecting these needs is changes in technology. Employers often scramble to find workers capable of implementing "hot" new technologies. Those with formal education or experience in information security, for example, are in demand because of the growing need for their skills and services. Another factor driving employers' needs is the timeframe during which projects must be completed.

Most community colleges and many independent technical institutes and proprietary schools offer associate's degrees in computer science or related information technology fields. Many of these programs may be geared toward meeting the needs of local businesses and are more occupation specific than are four-year degree programs. Some jobs may be better served by the level of training offered in such programs.

Employers usually look for people who have broad knowledge and experience related to computer systems and technologies, strong problem-solving and analytical skills, and good interpersonal skills. Courses in computer science or systems design offer good preparation for jobs in these occupations.

For jobs in a business environment, employers usually want systems analysts to have business management or closely related skills, while a background in the physical sciences, applied mathematics, or engineering is preferred for work in scientifically oriented organizations. Art or graphic design skills may be desirable for webmasters or Web developers.

Participation in internship or co-op programs offered by schools is another way to enhance employment opportunities. Many people develop advanced computer skills in noncomputer-related occupations and then transfer those skills to a computer field. For this reason, a background in the industry in which the person's job is located, such as financial services, banking, or accounting, can be important.

Others have taken computer science courses to supplement their study in fields such as accounting, inventory control, or other business areas. For example, a financial analyst who is proficient in computers might become a computer support specialist in financial systems development, while a computer programmer might move into a systems analyst job.

Computer systems analysts, database administrators, and computer scientists must be able to think logically and have good communication skills. Because they often deal with a number of tasks simultaneously, the ability to concentrate and pay close attention to detail is important. Although these computer specialists sometimes work independently, they frequently work in teams on large projects. They must be able to communicate effectively with computer personnel, such as programmers and managers, as well as with users or other staff who may have no technical computer background.

Technological advances come so rapidly in the computer field that continuous study is necessary to keep one's skills up-to-date.

Employers, hardware and software vendors, colleges and universities, and private training institutions offer continuing education. Additional training may come from professional development seminars offered by professional computing societies.

Computer Programmers

While there are many training paths available for programmers, the level of education and experience employers seek has been rising due to the growing number of qualified applicants and the specialization involved with most programming tasks. Bachelor's degrees are commonly required, although some programmers may qualify for certain jobs with two-year degrees or certificates. The associate's degree is an increasingly attractive entry-level credential for prospective computer programmers. Most community colleges and many independent technical institutes and proprietary schools offer an associate's degree in computer science or related information technology fields.

Employers are primarily interested in programming knowledge, and computer programmers can become certified in a programming language such as C++ or Java. College graduates who are interested in changing careers or developing an area of expertise also may return to a two-year community college or technical school for additional training.

In the absence of a degree, substantial specialized experience or expertise may be needed. Even when hiring programmers with a degree, employers appear to be placing more emphasis on previous experience.

Some computer programmers hold a college degree in computer science, mathematics, or information systems, whereas others have taken special courses in computer programming to supplement their degree in a field such as accounting, inventory control, or another area of business. As the level of education and training required by employers continues to rise, the proportion of programmers with a college degree should increase.

Required skills vary from job to job, but the demand for various skills generally is driven by changes in technology. Employers using computers for scientific or engineering applications usually prefer college graduates who have degrees in computer or information science, mathematics, engineering, or the physical sciences. Graduate degrees in related fields are required for some jobs. Employers who use computers for business applications prefer to hire people who have had college courses in MIS and business and who possess strong programming skills.

Although knowledge of traditional languages still is important, employers are placing increasing emphasis on newer, object-oriented programming languages and tools, such as C++ and Java. Additionally, employers are seeking persons familiar with fourth- and fifth-generation languages that involve graphic user interface (GUI) and systems programming. Employers also prefer applicants who have general business skills and experience related to the operations of the firm. Students can improve their employment prospects by participating in a college work-study program or by undertaking an internship.

Most systems programmers hold a four-year degree in computer science. Extensive knowledge of a variety of operating systems is essential for such workers. This includes being able to configure an operating system to work with different types of hardware and having the skills needed to adapt the operating system to best meet the needs of a particular organization. Systems programmers also must be able to work with database systems, such as DB2, Oracle, or Sybase.

When hiring programmers, employers look for people with the necessary programming skills who can think logically and pay close attention to detail. The job calls for patience, persistence, and the ability to perform exacting analytical work, especially under pressure. Ingenuity, creativity, and imagination also are particularly important when programmers design solutions and test their work for potential failures. The ability to work with abstract concepts and to do technical analysis is especially important for systems programmers because they work with the software that controls the computer's operation. Because programmers often work in teams and interact directly with users, employers want programmers able to communicate with nontechnical personnel.

Entry-level or junior programmers may work alone on simple assignments after some initial instruction, or they may be assigned to work on a team with more experienced programmers. Either way, beginning programmers generally must work under close supervision. Because technology changes so rapidly, programmers must continuously update their knowledge and skills by taking courses sponsored by their employer or by software vendors or offered through local community colleges and universities.

Certification

Certification is a way to demonstrate a level of competence in a particular field. Some product vendors or software firms offer certification and require professionals who work with their products to be certified. Many employers regard these certifications as the industry standard. For example, one method of acquiring enough knowledge to get a job as a database administrator is to become certified in a specific type of database management. The same is true for programmers.

Voluntary certification also is available through professional associations. For example, the Institute for Certification of Computer Professionals offers the designation Certified Computing Professional (CCP) to those who meet the institute's criteria for certification. The Quality Assurance Institute awards the designation Certified Quality Analyst (CQA) to those who meet education and experience requirements, pass an exam, and endorse a code of ethics. Neither designation is mandatory, but either may provide a job seeker with a competitive advantage.

Getting Ahead

Computer scientists employed in private industry may advance into managerial or project-leadership positions. Those employed in academic institutions can become heads of research departments or published authorities in their fields.

Systems analysts may be promoted to senior or lead systems analyst. Those who show leadership ability also can become project managers or advance into management positions, such as manager of information systems or chief information officer.

Database administrators may advance into management positions, such as chief technology officer, on the basis of their experience managing data and enforcing security.

Computer specialists with work experience and considerable expertise in a particular subject or a certain application may find lucrative opportunities as independent consultants or may choose to start their own computer consulting firms.

The prospects for advancement are good for skilled workers who keep up-to-date with the latest technology. In large organizations, programmers may be promoted to lead programmer and be given supervisory responsibilities. Some applications programmers may move into systems programming after they gain experience and take courses in systems software.

With general business experience, programmers may become programmer-analysts or systems analysts or be promoted to managerial positions. Other programmers who have specialized knowledge and experience with a language or operating system may work in research and development on multimedia or Internet technology, for example.

As employers increasingly contract out programming jobs, more opportunities should arise for experienced programmers with expertise in a specific area to work as consultants.

Earnings for Computer Professionals

Median annual earnings of computer systems analysts were $62,890 in 2002. The middle 50 percent earned between $49,500 and $78,350 a year. The lowest 10 percent earned less than $39,270, and the highest 10 percent earned more than $93,400. Median annual earnings in the industries employing the largest numbers of computer systems analysts in 2002 were as follows:

Federal government	$68,370
Computer systems design and related services	$67,690
Data processing, hosting, and related services	$64,560
Management of companies and enterprises	$63,390
Insurance carriers	$59,510

Median annual earnings of computer and information scientists in research were $77,760 in 2002. The middle 50 percent earned between $58,630 and $98,490. The lowest 10 percent earned less than $42,890, and the highest 10 percent earned more than $121,650. Median annual earnings of computer and information scientists employed in computer systems design and related services in 2002 were $78,730.

Median annual earnings of database administrators were $55,480 in 2002. The middle 50 percent earned between $40,550 and $75,100. The lowest 10 percent earned less than $30,750, and the highest 10 percent earned more than $92,910. In 2002, median annual earnings of database administrators employed in computer systems design and related services were $66,650, and, for those in management of companies and enterprises, earnings were $59,620.

Median annual earnings of computer programmers were $60,290 in 2002. The middle 50 percent earned between $45,960 and $78,140 a year. The lowest 10 percent earned less than $35,080, and the highest 10 percent earned more than $96,860.

Median annual earnings in the industries employing the largest numbers of computer programmers in 2002 were as follows:

Professional and commercial equipment and supplies merchant wholesalers	$70,440
Software publishers	$66,870
Computer systems design and related services	$65,640
Management of companies and enterprises	$59,850
Data processing, hosting, and related services	$59,300

According to the National Association of Colleges and Employers, starting offers for graduates with a master's degree in computer science averaged $62,806 in 2003. Starting offers averaged $47,109 for graduates with a bachelor's degree in computer science, $45,346 for those with a degree in computer programming, $41,118 for those with a degree in computer systems analysis, $40,556 for those with a degree in management information systems, and $38,282 for those with a degree in information sciences and systems.

According to Robert Half International, a firm providing specialized staffing services, average annual starting salaries in 2003 ranged from $51,500 to $80,500 for applications development programmer-analysts and from $55,000 to $87,750 for software developers. Average starting salaries for mainframe systems programmers ranged from $53,250 to $68,750 in 2003. Starting salaries in 2003 ranged from $69,750 to $101,750 for database administrators.

CHAPTER SIX

Forest Rangers

F orests and rangelands serve a variety of needs: they supply wood products, livestock, forage, minerals, and water; serve as sites for recreational activities; and provide habitat for wildlife.

Although much of the work is solitary, foresters and conservation scientists also deal regularly with landowners, loggers, forestry technicians and aides, farmers, ranchers, government officials, special-interest groups, and the public in general.

While some professionals in this category work out of doors, others work in offices or labs. The outdoor work can be physically demanding. There's the weather to deal with, and some foresters may need to walk long distances through heavily wooded areas to carry out their work.

Foresters may also work long hours fighting forest fires, and conservation scientists are called into the field to prevent erosion after a forest fire or to provide emergency assistance to control damage from floods or other natural disasters.

Job Titles in Forestry

There are several categories of workers that fall into this career area: foresters, range managers (also called range conservationists, range ecologists, or range scientists), conservation scientists, soil conservationists, forest rangers, park rangers, forestry technicians, and forest workers.

Foresters

Foresters manage forested land for a variety of purposes. They work for private timber companies or for county, state, or federal government forestry departments.

Timber Management. Those working in private industry may procure timber from private landowners. To do this, foresters contact local forest owners and gain permission to take inventory of the type, amount, and location of all standing timber on the property, a process known as timber cruising. Foresters then appraise the timber's worth, negotiate terms for removing the timber, and draw up a contract for procurement.

Next, they subcontract with loggers or pulpwood cutters for tree removal and aid in road layout. They also maintain close contact with the subcontractor's workers and the landowner to ensure that the work meets the landowner's requirements, as well as federal, state, and local environmental specifications.

Forestry consultants often act as agents for the forest owner, performing the above duties and negotiating timber sales with industrial procurement foresters.

Throughout the process, foresters consider the economics of the purchase as well as the environmental impact on natural resources, a function that has taken on added importance in recent years. To do this, they determine how best to conserve wildlife habitats, creek beds, water quality, and soil stability and how best to comply with environmental regulations. Foresters must balance the desire to conserve forested ecosystems for future generations with the need to use forest resources for recreational and economic purposes.

Regeneration. Foresters also supervise the planting and growing of new trees, a process called regeneration. They choose and prepare the site, using controlled burning, bulldozers, or herbicides to clear weeds, brush, and logging debris. They advise on the type, number, and placement of trees to be planted. Foresters then monitor the trees to ensure healthy growth and to determine the best time for harvesting. If they detect signs of disease or harmful insects, they decide on the best course of treatment to prevent contamination or infestation of healthy trees.

Public Use Management. Foresters who work for federal and state governments manage public forests and parks and work with private landowners to protect and manage forest land outside of the public domain. They may also design campgrounds and recreation areas.

Range Managers

Range managers—also called range conservationists, range ecologists, or range scientists—study, manage, improve, and protect rangelands to maximize their use without damaging the environment. Rangelands cover about one billion acres of the United States, mostly in the western states and Alaska. They contain many natural resources, including grass and shrubs for animal grazing, wildlife habitats, water from vast watersheds, recreation facilities, and valuable mineral and energy resources.

The duties of range managers may include keeping inventory of soils, plants, and animals; developing resource management plans; helping to restore degraded ecosystems; or assisting in managing a ranch. For example, they may help ranchers attain optimum livestock production by determining the number and kind of animals to graze, the grazing system to use, and the best season for grazing.

At the same time, however, range managers are concerned with maintaining soil stability and vegetation for other uses, such as wildlife habitat and outdoor recreation. They also plan and implement revegetation of disturbed sites.

Soil and Water Conservationists

Soil and water conservationists provide technical assistance to farmers, ranchers, forest managers, state and local agencies, and others concerned with the conservation of soil, water, and related natural resources. They develop programs for private landowners designed to make the most productive use of the land without damaging it.

Soil conservationists assist landowners by visiting areas with erosion problems, finding the source of the problem, and helping landowners and managers develop management practices to combat it.

Water conservationists assist private landowners and federal, state, and local governments by advising on a broad range of natural resource topics. These foresters specifically address issues of water quality, preserving water supplies, groundwater contamination, and management and conservation of water resources.

Working Conditions for Foresters

Working conditions for foresters vary considerably. Although some of the work is solitary, foresters and conservation scientists also deal regularly with landowners, loggers, forestry technicians and aides, farmers, ranchers, government officials, special-interest groups, and the public in general. Some foresters and conservation scientists work regular hours in offices or labs. Others may split their time between fieldwork and office work, while independent consultants and especially new, less-experienced workers spend the majority of their time outdoors overseeing or participating in hands-on work.

The work can be physically demanding. Some foresters and conservation scientists work outdoors in all types of weather, sometimes in isolated areas. Other foresters may need to walk long distances through densely wooded land to carry out their work. Foresters also may be involved with fighting fires. Conservation scientists often are called in to prevent erosion after a forest fire, and they provide emergency help after floods, mud slides, and tropical storms.

Qualifications and Training

Summer jobs may not require specific training, but if you're interested in a career in forestry, you'll want to consider earning a college degree.

Forestry

A bachelor's degree is usually the minimum requirement for any professional career in forestry. In the federal government, a combination of experience and appropriate education may occasionally substitute for a four-year degree, but the stiff job competition makes this difficult.

Sixteen states have mandatory licensing or voluntary registration requirements that a forester must meet in order to acquire the title professional forester and practice forestry in the state. Of those sixteen states, seven have mandatory licensing, five have mandatory registration, and the remaining four have optional registration. Both licensing and registration requirements usually entail completing a four-year degree in forestry and several years of forestry work experience. Candidates pursuing licensing also must pass a comprehensive written exam.

Foresters who wish to perform specialized research or teach should have an advanced degree, preferably a Ph.D.

Most land-grant colleges and universities offer bachelor's or higher degrees in forestry; about 110 of these degree programs at around fifty educational institutions are accredited by the Society of American Foresters. Curricula usually stress four components: ecology, measurement of forest resources, management of forest resources, and public policy. Students should balance general science courses such as ecology, biology, tree physiology, taxonomy, and soil formation with technical forestry courses, such as forest inventory, wildlife habitat assessment, remote sensing, land surveying, GPS technology, integrated forest resource management, silviculture, and forest protection. In addition, communications, mathematics, statistics, and computer science courses also are recommended.

Many forestry curricula include advanced computer applications such as GIS and resource assessment programs. Courses in resource policy and administration—specifically forest economics and business administration—supplement the student's scientific and technical knowledge. Forestry curricula increasingly include courses on optimal management practices, wetlands analysis, and sustainability and regulatory issues in response to the increasing focus on protecting forested lands during timber harvesting operations.

Prospective foresters should have a strong grasp of federal, state, and local policy issues and of increasingly numerous and complex environmental regulations that affect many forestry-related activities. Many colleges require students to complete a field session either in a camp operated by the college or in a cooperative work-study program with a federal or state agency or private industry. All schools encourage students to take summer jobs that provide experience in forestry or conservation work.

Range Management

A bachelor's degree in range management or range science is the standard minimum educational requirement for range managers; graduate degrees usually are required for teaching and research positions. More than thirty colleges and universities offer degrees in range management that are accredited by the Society of Range Management. A number of other schools offer degree programs in range science or in a closely related discipline with a range management or range science option.

Specialized range management courses combine plant, animal, and soil sciences with principles of ecology and resource management. Desirable electives include economics, statistics, forestry, hydrology, agronomy, wildlife, animal husbandry, computer science, and recreation. Selection of a minor in range management, such as wildlife ecology, watershed management, animal science, or agricultural economics, can often enhance qualifications for certain types of employment.

The Society for Range Management offers the Certified Professional Rangeland Manager (CPRM) designation. Candidates seeking this certificate must have a bachelor's degree in range science or a closely related field, have a minimum of five years of full-time work experience, and pass a comprehensive written exam.

Soil Conservation

Very few colleges and universities offer degrees in soil conservation. Most soil conservationists have degrees in environmental studies, agronomy, general agriculture, hydrology, or crop or soil science; a few have degrees in related fields such as wildlife biology, forestry, or range management. Programs of study usually include thirty semester hours in natural resources or agriculture, including at least three hours in soil science.

The Soil and Water Conservation Society sponsors a certification program based on education, experience, and testing. Completing the program confers the designation of Certified Professional Erosion and Sediment Control Specialist. The Soil and Water Conservation Society's address is listed in the Appendix.

The Job Outlook

Employment of conservation scientists and foresters is expected to grow more slowly than the average for all occupations through 2012. Growth should be strongest in private-sector consulting firms and in scientific research and development services. Demand will be spurred by a continuing emphasis on environmental protection, responsible land management, and water-related issues.

Job opportunities for conservation scientists will arise because government regulations, such as those regarding the management of storm water and coastlines, have created demand for persons knowledgeable about runoff and erosion on farms and in cities and suburbs. Soil- and water-quality experts will be needed as states design initiatives to improve water resources by preventing pollution caused by agricultural producers and industrial plants.

Fewer opportunities for conservation scientists and foresters are expected in federal and state government, mostly due to budgetary constraints and the trend among governments toward contracting functions out to private consulting firms. Also, federal land management agencies, such as the USDA Forest Service, have de-emphasized their timber programs and increasingly focused on wildlife, recreation, and sustaining ecosystems, thereby spurring demand for other life and social scientists rather than for foresters. However, departures of foresters who retire or leave the government for other reasons will result in some job openings between 2002 and 2012. A small number of new jobs will result from the need for range and soil conservationists to provide technical assistance to owners of grazing land through the Natural Resource Conservation Service.

Reductions in timber harvesting on public lands, most of which are located in the Northwest and California, also will dampen job growth for private-industry foresters in these regions. Opportunities will be better for foresters in the Southeast, where much forested land is privately owned. Salaried foresters working for private industry—such as paper companies, sawmills, and pulpwood mills—and consulting foresters will be needed to provide technical assistance and management plans to landowners.

Scientific research and development services have increased hiring of conservation scientists and foresters in recent years in response to demand for professionals to prepare environmental impact statements and erosion and sediment control plans, monitor water quality near logging sites, and advise on tree-harvesting practices required by federal, state, or local regulations. Hiring in these firms should continue during the 2002–12 period, although at a slower rate than over the last ten years.

Earnings for Foresters

In 2003, most bachelor's degree graduates entering the federal government as foresters, range managers, or soil conservationists started at $23,442 or $29,037, depending on academic achievement and experience. Those with a master's degree could start between $35,519 and $42,976; those with doctorates could start at $51,508. Beginning salaries were slightly higher in selected areas where the prevailing local pay level was higher. In 2003, the average federal salary for foresters in nonsupervisory, supervisory, and managerial positions was $59,233; for soil conservationists, $57,084; and for rangeland managers, $53,657.

According to the National Association of Colleges and Employers, graduates with a bachelor's degree in conservation and renewable natural resources received an average starting salary offer of $29,715 in 2003. In private industry, starting salaries for students with a bachelor's degree were comparable with starting salaries in the federal government, but starting salaries in state and local governments were usually lower. Conservation scientists and foresters who work for federal, state, and local governments and large private firms generally receive more generous benefits than do those working for smaller firms.

Median annual earnings of conservation scientists were $50,340 in 2002. The middle 50 percent earned between $39,300 and $61,440. The lowest 10 percent earned less than $30,630, and the highest 10 percent earned more than $70,770.

Median annual earnings of foresters were $46,730 in 2002. The middle 50 percent earned between $36,330 and $56,890. The lowest 10 percent earned less than $29,690, and the highest 10 percent earned more than $69,600.

Jobs in the National Park Service

The National Park Service, a bureau under the U.S. Department of the Interior, administers more than 350 sites. These encompass natural and recreational areas across the country, including the Grand Canyon, Yellowstone National Park, and Lake Mead. The National Park Service provides a variety of opportunities for people interested in working on their own in the great outdoors.

Because most sites are not located near major cities, serious candidates must, for the most part, be prepared to relocate. Housing may or may not be provided, depending upon the site and the position.

Park Rangers

The National Park Service employs both a permanent and seasonal workforce to protect resources and to serve the public. Park rangers are hired to work in one of three categories, though job duties often overlap.

Law Enforcement. Park rangers in the law enforcement category provide safety for visitors by patrolling park roads and visitor areas. They also may provide interpretive and other information as well as respond to emergency situations.

Interpretation. Duties vary greatly from position to position and site to site, but rangers in the interpretation division are usually responsible for developing and presenting programs that explain a park's historic, cultural, or archaeological features. This is done through talks, demonstrations, and guided walking tours. Rangers also sit at information desks, provide visitor services, or participate in conservation or restoration projects. Entry-level employees might also collect fees, provide first aid, and operate audiovisual equipment.

General Duty. Individuals interested in and qualified for forestry and related fields would be placed in this category with the National Park Service. General-duty park rangers perform a variety of services, which may include fee collection and law enforcement. Those with appropriate backgrounds work in backcountry, campground, recreation, forest or resource management areas.

Other responsibilities within parks or conservation areas might include conservation and restoration activities, fire control, wildlife management, and insect or plant disease control.

Qualifications and Salaries

The National Park Service weighs several factors in determining a candidate's eligibility for employment and at which salary level he or she is placed. In general, those with the least experience or education begin at the lowest federal government salary grade, which is GS-2. The requirements for this grade are only six months of experience in related work or a high school diploma or its equivalency.

The more related work experience or education an applicant has, the higher the salary level. For example, GS-4 requires eighteen months of general experience in park operations or in related fields and six months of specialized experience or one ninety-day season as a seasonal park ranger at the GS-3 level.

Completion of two academic years of college may be substituted for experience if the course work covered is related to the duties of a park ranger.

Getting Your Foot in the Door

Competition for jobs, especially at the most well-known sites, can be fierce. But the National Park Service employs a huge permanent staff, which is supplemented tenfold by an essential seasonal work force during peak visitation periods.

The best way for a newcomer to break in is to start with seasonal employment during school breaks. Permanent employment will be easier to secure once you have completed two or three summer seasons.

Based on the Office of Personnel Management regulations, veterans of the U.S. Armed Forces have a decided advantage. Depending upon their experience, they may be given preference among applicants.

How to Apply

Recruitment for summer employment begins September 1 with a January 15 deadline. Some sites, such as Death Valley or Everglades National Park, also have a busy winter season. The winter recruitment period is June 1 through July 15.

Applications for seasonal employment with the National Park Service can be obtained through the Office of Personnel Management or by writing to:

U.S. Department of the Interior
National Park Service
Seasonal Employment Unit
PO Box 37127
Washington, DC 20013

You may also contact one of the nine regional offices of the National Park Service, which are listed in the Appendix.

Parks Canada

Throughout Canada, national parks, historic sites, marine conservation areas, and historic canals are maintained to protect their representation of the natural and marine regions of the country, particularly those that reflect Canada's cultural diversity. Parks Canada is the government agency mandated to oversee these national sites.

Park Wardens

Parks Canada employs approximately four hundred park wardens, whose responsibilities include protecting and managing natural resources, providing scientific information, and administering public safety programs.

Park wardens work in a variety of national parks or historic sites across the country. Their work environment varies depending on the location of the site.

Regardless of where a park warden works, he or she will most likely live in a small community in or adjacent to the park, since very few national parks are near large cities.

Park wardens interact with the local people and organizations that are involved in the park's management and operations. They work with local people who have an intimate knowledge of the area and its resources based on personal experiences and generations of traditional knowledge. This knowledge and experience is valuable and a strong consideration in management of the park.

Qualifications and Training

The minimum educational requirement to become a park warden is a university degree in sciences or natural resources.

The park warden's duties require a good level of physical fitness and the ability to travel and work in a variety of terrestrial and marine environments. Experience in wilderness travel using a variety of personal and technical equipment and techniques (such as hiking, canoeing, or snowmobiling) is required. Additional requirements include hands-on experience in natural resources management, public safety, or building community relationships.

Although park wardens often live in secluded settings, they must be able to establish partnerships and communicate and interact effectively with a variety of people. Other basic qualifications include a valid driver's license, valid first-aid and CPR certificates, pleasure craft operator license, and successful completion of the Canadian firearms safety course. A pre-employment medical exam and a security check are also required.

Parks Canada Opportunities for Students

Each year, Parks Canada offers more than a thousand jobs to full-time students in secondary schools, colleges, technical institutes, and universities. Jobs generally run from May to September and are available in areas such as the warden service, visitor services, assistance on the waterways, interpretive activities, systems work, and office support. These summer jobs afford students the opportunity to learn about Parks Canada and the federal government. Students also gain valuable work experience and learn skills that will improve their future employment prospects.

To be eligible for summer employment, students must meet the following criteria: be a full-time secondary or postsecondary student in an accredited institution; plan to return to full-time studies in the next academic term; and be of the minimum age to work in the province where the job is located.

Students who have worked for Parks Canada are often rehired the following summer by the same park or site. To be considered for re-employment, students must continue to meet the eligibility criteria and have worked in a student job with Parks Canada within the past year.

Compensation for student jobs is based on rates established by Parks Canada in keeping with the federal government's student programs. If travel and accommodation expenses are incurred, they are paid by the agency.

What's It's Really Like

Following is the account of a professional forester. See whether his career might be of interest to you.

Dr. Ronald Miller, Independent Consultant

Dr. Ronald Miller is a specialist in biodiversity conservation planning. He works for Pioneer Geographic Designs in Northampton, Massachusetts, a firm involved in providing environmental planning assistance at the international, national, regional, and local levels. The company specializes in the use of computerized information technologies, including the design and creation of maps and databases.

Dr. Miller has an impressive list of educational credentials: a B.A. in environmental sciences from Brandeis University in Waltham, Massachusetts; an M.S. in forestry and wildlife ecology from the University of Florida in Gainesville; further graduate study in the department of biological sciences at Harvard University; and a Ph.D. from the Institute of Ecology at the University of Georgia in Athens. He has been working steadily in the field since earning his doctorate.

On the Job. "Field science interested me at an early age," Dr. Miller says. "I have always wanted to work with and for the protection of plants and animals."

Working as a consultant, Dr. Miller focuses on many different categories of biological conservation in various regions of the world. His work often involves long hours of preparation when he writes reports. He works independently and is generally able to conduct the work in the way that he finds most effective.

"The most enjoyable part of the work is being able to travel to many different regions," says Dr. Miller. "For example, I recently gave a presentation of my work at the annual meeting of the International Union of Forestry Research Organizations in Tampere, Finland.

"The most difficult part of being a consultant is having to go through sometimes long periods without income. For example, I have gone through almost one year without a paid position. Also, I must provide myself with health insurance and retirement, both of which are expensive."

Advice from Dr. Miller. Dr. Miller has some words of encouragement for aspiring foresters. "If possible, you should identify what you are most interested in while you are in college. Then you should apply for any significant opportunities that you become aware of that will allow you to gain experience in this field. Don't think that any opportunities that you see advertised are too good for someone like yourself—go for it."

For More Information

Periodicals

Job Seeker lists vacancies in forestry, forest products, wildlife, fisheries, range, biology, environmental protection and education, recreation, parks, and other natural resource fields. Advertisers include timber industries, forest consultants, nurseries, federal and state agencies, universities, nature centers, and other related organizations. To obtain a subscription, write to:

Job Seeker
403 Oakwood Street
Warrens, WI 54666

Journal of Forestry is a monthly publication listing both positions wanted and positions available. It is free to members of the Society of American Foresters or for a fee to subscribers. For more information, contact:

Society of American Foresters
5400 Grosvenor Lane
Bethesda, MD 20814
www.safnet.org

National Environmental Employment Report is an informative monthly newsletter including current job listings and articles and insight on careers in the environmental world. For more information, contact:

Environmental Career Center
2 Eaton Street, Suite 711
Hampton, VA 23669
www.environmentalcareer.com

The Environmental Careers Organization provides information and links to a variety of opportunities for internships in environmental careers. For more information, contact:

Environmental Careers Organization
30 Winter Street
Boston, MA 02108
www.eco.org

The National Wildlife Federation's *Conservation Directory* is updated annually and lists by states and Canadian provinces the organizations, agencies, and officials concerned with natural resource use and management. Learn more by visiting the website at www.nwf.org.

Books
The following books provide additional information about jobs for people interested in forestry and environmental careers:

DeGalan, Julie and Bryon Middlekauf. *Great Jobs for Environmental Studies Majors.* New York: McGraw-Hill, 2002.

Fasulo, Michael. *Careers for Environmental Types*, 2nd edition. New York: McGraw-Hill, 2001.

Miller, Louise. *Careers for Nature Lovers*, 2nd edition. New York: McGraw-Hill, 2001.

CHAPTER SEVEN

Security Guards

uards, who are also called security officers, patrol and inspect property to protect against fire, theft, vandalism, terrorism, and illegal activity. These workers protect their employer's investment, enforce laws within the property, and deter criminal activity or other potential problems. They use radio and telephone communications to call for assistance from police, fire, or emergency medical services as the situation dictates. Security guards write comprehensive reports outlining their observations and activities during their assigned shifts. They may also interview witnesses and victims, prepare case reports, and testify in court.

Job Settings and Responsibilities

Although all security guards perform many of the same duties, specific duties vary based on whether the guard works in a static security position or on a mobile patrol. Guards assigned to static security positions usually serve the client at one location for a specific length of time. These guards must become closely acquainted with both the property and the people associated with it and often monitor alarms and closed-circuit television cameras. In contrast, guards assigned to mobile-patrol duty drive or walk from location to location and conduct security checks within an assigned geographic zone. They may detain or arrest criminal violators, answer service calls concerning criminal activity or problems, and issue warnings for traffic violations.

Specific job responsibilities also vary with the size, type, and location of the employer. In department stores, guards protect people, records, merchandise, money, and equipment. They often work with undercover store detectives to prevent theft by customers or store employees and help in the apprehension of shoplifting suspects prior to arrival by police. Some shopping centers hire security officers mounted on horses or bicycles to patrol parking lots to help deter car theft and robberies.

In office buildings, banks, and hospitals, guards maintain order and protect property, staff, and customers.

At air, sea, and rail terminals and other transportation facilities, guards protect people, freight, property, and equipment. They may screen passengers and visitors for weapons and explosives using metal detectors and high-tech equipment, ensure nothing is stolen while being loaded or unloaded, and watch for fires and criminal activity.

Guards who work in public buildings such as museums or art galleries protect paintings and exhibits by inspecting people and packages entering and leaving the building.

In factories, laboratories, government buildings, data processing centers, and military bases, security officers protect information, products, computer codes, and defense secrets and check the credentials of people and vehicles entering and leaving the premises.

Guards working at universities, parks, and sports stadiums perform crowd control, supervise parking and seating, and direct traffic. Security guards stationed at the entrance to bars and places of adult entertainment, such as nightclubs, prevent access by minors, collect cover charges at the door, maintain order among customers, and protect property and patrons.

Armored-car guards protect money and valuables during transit. In addition, they protect individuals responsible for making commercial bank deposits from theft or bodily injury. When the armored car arrives at the door of a business, an armed guard enters, signs for the money, and returns to the truck with the valuables in hand. Carrying money between the truck and the business

SECURITY GUARDS · 121

can be extremely hazardous for guards. Because of this risk, armored-car guards usually wear bullet-proof vests.

Gaming surveillance officers and gaming investigators act as security agents for casino managers and patrons. They observe casino operations for irregular activities, such as cheating or theft, by either employees or patrons. To do this, surveillance officers and investigators often monitor activities from a catwalk over one-way mirrors located above the casino floor. Many casinos use audio and video equipment, allowing surveillance officers and investigators to observe these same areas via monitors. Audio and videotapes are kept as a record and are sometimes used as evidence against alleged criminals in police investigations.

Working Conditions

Most security guards spend considerable time on their feet, either assigned to a specific post or patrolling buildings and grounds. Guards may be stationed at a guard desk inside a building to monitor electronic security and surveillance devices or to check the credentials of persons entering or leaving the premises. They also may be stationed at a guardhouse outside the entrance to a gated facility or community and use a portable radio or cellular telephone that allows them to be in constant contact with a central station.

The work usually is routine, but guards must be constantly alert for threats to themselves or to the property they are protecting. Guards who work during the day may have a great deal of contact with other employees and members of the public.

Gaming surveillance often takes place behind a bank of monitors controlling several cameras in a casino, which can cause eyestrain.

Guards usually work eight-hour shifts for forty hours per week and often are on call in case an emergency arises. Some employers operate three shifts, and guards rotate to equally divide daytime, weekend, and holiday work. Guards usually eat on the job instead of taking a regular break away from the site. More than one in seven guards work part-time. For many individuals guard work is a second job to supplement their primary earnings.

Qualifications and Training

Most states require that guards be licensed. To be licensed as a guard, individuals must usually be at least eighteen years old, pass a background check, and complete classroom training in such subjects as property rights, emergency procedures, and detention of suspected criminals. Drug testing often is required and may be random and ongoing.

Many employers of unarmed guards have no specific educational requirements. For armed guards, employers usually prefer individuals who are high school graduates or hold an equivalent certification. Many jobs require a driver's license.

For positions as armed guards, employers often seek people who have had responsible experience in other occupations. Guards who carry weapons must be licensed by the appropriate government authority, and some receive further certification as special police officers, which allows them to make limited types of arrests while on duty. Armed-guard positions involve more stringent background checks and entry requirements than those of unarmed guards because of greater insurance liability risks. Compared to unarmed security guards, armed guards and special police typically enjoy higher earnings and benefits, greater job security, more advancement potential, and usually are given more training and responsibility.

Rigorous hiring and screening programs consisting of background, criminal-record, and fingerprint checks are becoming the norm in the occupation. Applicants are expected to have good character references, no serious police record, and good health. They should be mentally alert, emotionally stable, and physically fit in order to cope with emergencies. Guards who have frequent contact with the public should be able to communicate well.

The amount of training guards receive varies. Training requirements are higher for armed guards because their employers are legally responsible for any use of force. Armed guards receive formal training in areas such as weapons retention and laws covering the use of force.

Many employers give newly hired guards instruction before they start the job and also provide on-the-job training. An increasing number of states are making ongoing training a legal requirement for retention of certification. Guards may receive training in protection, public relations, report writing, crisis deterrence, and first aid, as well as specialized training relevant to their particular assignments.

Guards employed at establishments placing a heavy emphasis on security usually receive extensive formal training. For example, guards at nuclear power plants undergo several months of training before being placed on duty under close supervision. They are taught to use firearms, administer first aid, operate alarm systems and electronic security equipment, and spot and deal with potential security problems. Guards authorized to carry firearms may be periodically tested in their use.

Although guards in small companies may receive periodic salary increases, advancement opportunities are limited. Most large organizations use a military type of ranking that offers the possibility of advancement in position and salary. Some guards may advance to supervisor or security manager positions. Guards with management skills may open their own contract security agencies.

In addition to the keen observation skills required to perform their jobs, gaming surveillance officers and gaming investigators must have excellent verbal and writing abilities to document violations or suspicious behavior. They also need to be physically fit and have quick reflexes because they sometimes must detain individuals until local law enforcement officials arrive on the scene.

Surveillance officers and investigators usually do not need a bachelor's degree, but some training beyond high school is required; previous security experience is a plus. Several educational institutions offer certification programs. Training classes usually are conducted using surveillance-camera equipment.

Desirable Traits

All security officers must show good judgment and common sense, follow directions and directives from supervisors, accurately testify in court, and follow company policies and guidelines. Guards should have a professional appearance and attitude and be able to interact with the public. They also must be able to take charge and direct others in emergencies or other dangerous situations.

In a large organization, the security manager is often in charge of a trained guard force divided into shifts; in a small organization, a single worker may be responsible for all security.

The Job Outlook

Opportunities for security guards are expected to be favorable in the future. Numerous job openings will stem from employment growth attributable to the desire for increased security and from the need to replace those who leave this large occupation each year.

In addition to full-time job opportunities, the limited training requirements and flexible hours attract many people seeking part-time work or second jobs. However, significant competition is expected for higher-paying positions that require longer periods of training. These positions usually are found at facilities that require a high level of security, such as nuclear power plants or weapons installations.

Employment of security guards and gaming surveillance officers is expected to grow faster than the average for all occupations through 2012 as concern about crime, vandalism, and terrorism continue to increase the need for security. Demand for guards also will grow as private firms increasingly perform security duties, such as monitoring crowds at airports and providing security in courts, jobs that were formerly handled by government police officers and marshals.

Because enlisting the services of a security firm is easier and less costly than assuming direct responsibility for hiring, training, and managing a security guard force, job growth is expected to be concentrated among contract security agencies.

Casinos will continue to hire more surveillance officers as more states legalize gambling and as the number of casinos increases in states where gambling is already legal. Additionally, casino security forces will employ more technically trained personnel as technology becomes increasingly important in thwarting casino cheating and theft.

Earnings

Median annual earnings of security guards were $19,140 in 2002. The middle 50 percent earned between $15,910 and $23,920. The lowest 10 percent earned less than $13,740, and the highest 10 percent earned more than $31,540. Median annual earnings in the industries employing the largest numbers of security guards in 2002 were as follows:

Elementary and secondary schools	$24,470
General medical and surgical hospitals	$24,050
Local governments	$22,120
Traveler accommodations	$21,390
Investigation and security services	$17,910

Gaming surveillance officers and gaming investigators had median annual earnings of $23,110 in 2002. The middle 50 percent earned between $19,620 and $28,420. The lowest 10 percent earned less than $15,930, and the highest 10 percent earned more than $35,170.

....

What It's Really Like

Read the story of a professional security guard to find out whether you might be interested in this line of work.

Timothy T. Speed Jr., Security Supervisor

Timothy Speed is the security supervisor for a large apartment complex in Oklahoma City, Oklahoma. He has worked in this field since 1994.

The complex where Timothy works is usually considered a one-officer post, which is a location that requires only one officer for security. On weekends, however, the post often has up to three officers on duty.

As Timothy describes it, "The atmosphere is mostly quiet on one-officer posts. Most days are a bit on the boring side. There are many times when you do nothing more than sit, stand, or patrol your post, and nothing happens. Then there are days you are so busy you wonder where the time went."

Timothy reports that working as a security officer at an apartment complex can be stressful because of the need to keep peace among the tenants. The security staff handles complaints about loud noise and domestic disturbances. As Timothy says, "These types of calls seem to build, with everything being quiet for months at a time, and then the tension breaks and everything goes wild.

"There are times that it can be very dangerous. Some people, who are not the most law abiding to begin with, think that we security officers don't have the right to tell them what to do. Some of them would just as soon kill you as look at you.

"But really, most of the people are nice. The upside is that you get to meet a lot of people from all walks of life."

Timothy talks about the financial realities of the job: "The downside to this work is that there is very little upward momentum. . . . With most security agencies I have worked for, you are lucky to get minimum wage.

"Here on this job, though, if you work full-time, you get a salary and an apartment. Part-time officers work thirteen hours a week in exchange for an apartment. All officers are required to live on the property in case something big happens."

How Timothy Got Started. Timothy's interest in security work was a direct result of his desire to help others. As he describes it: "I wanted to do something to help people, and what better way to help people than to make them feel safe in their own homes and office buildings? The first security job I got was through a friend of mine whom I met at the local gun range. She was leaving a position with a security agency to start a job as a corrections officer. I applied and got the job, with my friend's recommendation, of course."

Timothy explains that in Oklahoma, all security officers must complete a training program to be fully licensed. Once he had a conditional license, Timothy attended training for an unarmed license. The program is forty hours long, and successful completion requires perfect attendance and a score of at least 80 percent on six tests.

Timothy has also had training for certification with an ASP baton, an expandable night stick. He has also been trained for licensure as an armed security officer. In addition, he has completed training to carry both a semiautomatic pistol and a twelve-gauge pump shotgun.

Advice from Timothy Speed. Timothy offers some realistic advice to aspiring security officers: "Firstly, my advice to anyone entering this field is to use the experience as nothing more than a stepping-stone to bigger and better things. A career as a police officer would be a good place to take this. In this field as a security officer, you sometimes will be placed in situations that not even some police officers would want to find themselves in, and this provides practical experience for any law enforcement position.

"Secondly, always treat the people you deal with the way you would want to be treated, but also keep them at a distance— because no human being is predictable. In essence, I am saying to treat every person as a possible threat.

"Lastly, if you can help it, never work an unarmed post because the firearm at your side is a great deterrent to would-be criminals. As a safety precaution, I suggest you purchase a bulletproof vest and wear it at all times while on duty.

"Always be alert, even if it's been quiet for months, because this is when things start to happen. Always, no matter what the person you are dealing with calls you, keep a professional attitude and perspective on the job. If you let them get to you, you have most definitely lost the battle and let them win.

"And you should realize that most security positions are worked at night, forty hours a week, including weekends, so if you're in this field, be prepared to give up weekends because that is when our job is done."

For More Information

Further information about work opportunities for guards is available from local security and guard firms and state employment service offices. Information about licensing requirements for guards may be obtained from the state licensing commission or the state police department. In states where local jurisdictions establish the licensing requirements, contact a local government authority such as the sheriff, county executive, or city manager.

CHAPTER EIGHT

Mail Carriers

E ach week, the U.S. Postal Service delivers billions of pieces of mail, including letters, bills, advertisements, and packages. To do this in an efficient and timely manner, the postal service employs about 845,000 workers. Most of these workers are postal clerks, who sort mail and serve customers in post offices, or mail carriers, who deliver the mail.

Clerks and carriers are distinguished by the type of work they do. Clerks are usually classified by the mail-processing function they perform, whereas carriers are classified by their type of route, city or rural.

Postal Clerks

About 350 mail processing centers throughout the country service post offices in surrounding areas and are staffed primarily by postal clerks. Postal service clerks, also known as window clerks, sell stamps, money orders, stationery, and mailing envelopes and boxes. They also weigh packages to determine postage and check that packages are in satisfactory condition for mailing. These clerks register, certify, and insure mail and answer questions about postage rates, post office boxes, mailing restrictions, and other postal matters. Window clerks also help customers file claims for damaged packages.

Other clerks, known as mail sorters, processors, and processing machine operators, prepare incoming and outgoing mail for distribution. These workers are commonly referred to as mail handlers, distribution clerks, mail processors, or mail processing clerks. They load and unload postal trucks and move mail around the processing center with forklifts, small electric tractors, or hand-pushed carts. They also load and operate mail processing, sorting, and canceling machinery.

Mail Carriers

Once mail has been processed and sorted, it is delivered by mail carriers. Carriers are classified by the type of route, either city or rural, but their general duties are similar. Most carriers deliver and collect mail along established routes. They start work at the post office early in the morning, when they arrange the mail in delivery sequence. Automated equipment has reduced the time that carriers need to sort the mail, allowing them to spend more time delivering it.

Mail carriers cover their routes on foot, by vehicle, or a combination of both. On foot, they carry a heavy load of mail in a satchel or push it on a cart. In most urban and rural areas, they use a car or small truck. Although the postal service provides vehicles to city carriers, most rural carriers must use their own automobiles. Deliveries are made house-to-house, to roadside mailboxes, and to large buildings such as offices or apartments, which generally have all of their tenants' mailboxes in one location.

Besides delivering and collecting mail, carriers collect money for postage-due and cash-on-delivery (COD) fees and obtain signed receipts for registered, certified, and insured mail. If a customer is not home, the carrier leaves a notice that tells where special mail is being held. After completing their routes, carriers return to the post office with mail gathered from street collection boxes, homes, and businesses and turn in the mail, receipts, and money collected during the day.

Some city carriers may have specialized duties, such as delivering only parcels or picking up mail from mail collection boxes. In contrast to city carriers, rural carriers provide a wider range of postal services in addition to delivering and picking up mail. For example, rural carriers may sell stamps and money orders and register, certify, and insure parcels and letters. All carriers, however, must be able to answer customers' questions about postal regulations and services and provide change-of-address cards and other postal forms when requested.

Qualifications and Training

Postal service workers must be at least eighteen years old and must be U.S. citizens or have been granted permanent resident-alien status in the United States. Male employees must have registered with the Selective Service upon reaching age eighteen.

Applicants should have a basic competency in English. Qualification is based on a written examination that measures speed and accuracy at checking names and numbers and the ability to memorize mail distribution procedures. Applicants must pass a physical examination and drug test and may be asked to show that they can lift and handle mail sacks weighing seventy pounds. Applicants for mail carrier positions must have a driver's license and a good driving record and must receive a passing grade on a road test.

Exam schedules can be obtained from individual post offices or mail processing centers; applicants should inquire at the facility where they wish to work. Applicants' names are listed in order of their examination scores. Five points are added to the score of an honorably discharged veteran, and ten points are added to the score of a veteran who was wounded in combat or is disabled. When a vacancy occurs, the appointing officer chooses one of the top three applicants; the rest of the names remain on the list to be considered for future openings until their eligibility expires, usually two years after the examination date.

Relatively few people become postal clerks or mail carriers as a first job because of keen competition and the customary waiting period of one to two years or more after passing the examination. It is not surprising, therefore, that most entrants transfer from other occupations.

New postal service workers are trained on the job by experienced workers. Many post offices provide classroom instruction on safety and defensive driving. Workers receive additional instruction when new equipment or procedures are introduced. In these cases, workers usually are trained by another postal employee or a training specialist.

A good memory and the ability to read rapidly and accurately are important. Postal clerks and mail carriers should be courteous and tactful when dealing with the public, especially when answering questions or receiving complaints. Good interpersonal skills also are vital because mail distribution clerks work closely with other postal workers, frequently under the tension and strain of meeting dispatch or transportation deadlines and quotas.

Postal service workers often begin on a part-time, flexible basis and become regular or full-time in order of seniority, as vacancies occur. Full-time workers may bid for preferred assignments, such as the day shift or a high-level nonsupervisory position. Carriers can look forward to obtaining preferred routes as their seniority increases. Postal service workers can advance to supervisory positions on a competitive basis.

The Job Outlook

Those seeking a job in the U.S. Postal Service can expect to encounter keen competition. The number of applicants for postal clerk and mail carrier positions is expected to continue to far exceed the number of openings due to low entry requirements and attractive wages and benefits.

Employment of postal service workers is expected to decline through 2012. Still, many jobs will become available because of the need to replace workers who retire or leave the occupation.

A small decline in employment is expected among window clerks through 2012. Efforts by the postal service to provide better service may somewhat increase the demand for window clerks, but this demand will be offset by the use of electronic communications technologies and private delivery companies. Employment of mail sorters, processors, and processing machine operators is expected to decline because of the increasing use of automated materials handling equipment and optical character readers, bar code sorters, and other automated sorting equipment.

Several factors are expected to influence demand for mail carriers. The competition from alternative delivery systems and new forms of electronic communication could decrease the total volume of mail handled. Most of the decrease is expected to be in first-class mail, but an increase in package deliveries is expected due to the rising number of purchases made through the Internet.

Although total mail volume may decrease, the number of addresses to which mail must be delivered will continue to grow. However, increased use of the "delivery point sequencing" system, which allows machines to sort mail directly into the order of delivery, should continue to reduce the amount of time that carriers spend sorting mail, allowing them to handle longer routes.

In addition, the postal service is moving toward more centralized mail delivery, such as the use of cluster boxes, to cut down on the number of door-to-door deliveries. These trends are expected to increase carrier productivity, resulting in a small decline in employment among mail carriers. The increasing number of delivery points may result in greater demand for rural mail carriers than for city mail carriers because much of the increase in delivery points will be seen in less-urbanized areas.

Currently, the role of the U.S. Postal Service as a government-approved monopoly is a topic of debate. Any legislative changes that would privatize or deregulate the postal service might affect employment of all its workers. Employment and schedules in the postal service fluctuate with the demand for its services. When mail volume is high, full-time workers work overtime, part-time workers get additional hours, and casual workers may be hired. When mail volume is low, overtime is curtailed, part-timers work fewer hours, and casual workers are discharged.

Earnings

Median annual earnings of postal mail carriers were $39,530 in 2002. The middle 50 percent earned between $36,020 and $43,040. The lowest 10 percent had earnings of less than $31,180, while the top 10 percent earned over $47,500. Rural mail carriers are reimbursed for mileage put on their own vehicles while delivering mail.

Median annual earnings of postal service clerks were $39,700 in 2002. The middle 50 percent earned between $37,160 and $42,230. The lowest 10 percent had earnings of less than $35,640, while the top 10 percent earned more than $43,750.

Median annual earnings of mail sorters, processors, and processing machine operators were $38,150 in 2002. The middle 50 percent earned between $30,140 and $41,450. The lowest 10 percent had earnings of less than $21,680, while the top 10 percent earned more than $43,430.

Postal service workers enjoy a variety of employer-provided benefits similar to those enjoyed by federal government workers. The American Postal Workers Union, the National Association of Letter Carriers, the National Postal Mail Handlers Union, and the National Rural Letter Carriers Association together represent most of these workers.

Related Fields

Others with duties related to those of mail carriers include messengers, merchandise deliverers, and delivery-route truck drivers. Employers include major parcel delivery companies such as United Parcel Service and Federal Express as well as local, regional, and national delivery companies. Most major cities have interoffice delivery companies that employ bicycle riders to deliver packages within the downtown area.

What It's Really Like

Read about the experiences of a veteran mail carrier to see whether you might like to pursue this career.

Nick Delia, Letter Carrier

Nick Delia and his wife are both letter carriers. Nick has been working for the U.S. Postal Service for more than fifteen years.

On the Job. One of the most important qualifications for the job, according to Nick, is a good memory. "You have to rely on your memory a lot in this job," he says. "You get to know who is living at a certain address, who's a forward. Forwarding the mail is the responsibility of the letter carrier."

Nick's route is primarily a business route, which means that he is in and out of his truck many times each day. "For example, the local newspaper is on my route," he explains. "I pull up to the building, take out their buckets of mail, take them into the mail room, then get back into the truck and go to the next stop."

Nick's workday starts at 6:00 A.M. Most of the mail is already at the post office when he arrives, having been handled by clerks who arrive at 4:00 A.M. Nick's first duty is to count the mail for his route, in order to determine how long it will take to deliver it. The mail is kept in trays that each contain two feet of letter-size envelopes, plus magazines and newspapers. On Nick's route, he can deliver fifteen feet of mail in an eight-hour shift. If there is more mail than that on a given day, he needs to request help or else work overtime.

After counting the mail, Nick inspects each item, checking for forwarded pieces or those that should be held at the post office. He then puts the mail into a large case that has compartments for the different delivery locations.

Nick keeps a written record of certified or registered mail, since he must obtain a signature upon delivery of these items. He also looks for mark-up mail, which is any item that has been marked "moved, left no forwarding address" or "attempted, addressee unknown." After this is complete, Nick takes the mail out of the compartmentalized case in the order in which it will be delivered. He bundles it in rubber bands and loads it into his truck.

This preparation work takes about four hours every day. Nick usually starts his route by 10:00 A.M. As he says, "It looks like the easiest job in the world, but most people have no idea what goes on behind the scenes. The delivery part is the easiest part of the day.

"But, of course, you have a lot to deal with on the street. That old saying, 'neither snow, nor sleet' and all that is really true. It doesn't matter what the weather is; the mail has to go."

Mail carriers do have the opportunity to work a good deal of overtime. Nick says that while it can even be possible to earn an additional $10,000 a year in overtime pay, the carriers certainly work for their money. "Not in every job do you have a dog chasing you down the street or find yourself working through a lightning storm. And we have traffic to deal with, too, and kids running out in the street. We've got our hazards.

"But basically, I think it's a good job. I get a feeling of accomplishment on my job. At the beginning of the day there's mail everywhere, but by the end of the day, there's nothing left; it's done. And I enjoy working outside, which is half of the job. I couldn't be a clerk, working indoors all day."

Advice from Nick Delia. Nick offers some advice based on his years of working as a mail carrier: "You've got to be physically fit. In addition, this is basically an unskilled job. Of course, you need a good memory and have to be intelligent, but if a person is not inclined to go to college, then this would be a good job."

Professional Associations

For more information on the careers covered in this book, contact the appropriate professional associations or related resource listed below.

Writers

Information about careers in writing can be obtained from:

American Society of Journalists and Authors
1501 Broadway, Suite 302
New York, NY 10036
www.asja.org

Society of American Travel Writers
1500 Sunday Drive, Suite 102
Raleigh, NC 27607
www.satw.org

For information on finding an agent, contact:

Association of Authors' Representatives, Inc.
PO Box 237202, Ansonia Station
New York, NY 10003
www.aar-online.org

Literary Market Place
Information Today, Inc.
143 Old Marlton Pike
Medford, NJ 08055
www.literarymarketplace.com
   A book and website listing publishers and agents in the United States and Canada

For information on college internships in magazine editing, contact:

American Society of Magazine Editors
810 Seventh Avenue, Twenty-Fourth Floor
New York, NY 10019
www.magazine.org/Editorial

For information on careers in technical writing, contact:

Society for Technical Communication
901 North Stuart Street, Suite 904
Arlington, VA 22203
www.stc.org

General career information is available from:

Newspaper Association of America
1921 Gallows Road, Suite 600
Vienna, VA 22182
www.naa.org

Information on careers in journalism, colleges and universities that offer degree programs in journalism or communications, and journalism scholarships and internships may be obtained from:

The Dow Jones Newspaper Fund
PO Box 300
Princeton, NJ 08543
http://djnewspaperfund.dowjones.com/fund

For a list of junior and community colleges offering programs in journalism, contact:

Community College Journalism Association
163 East Loop Drive
Camarillo, CA 93010
www.ccjaonline.org

Information on union wage rates for newspaper and magazine reporters is available from:

The Newspaper Guild
501 Third Street NW, Suite 250
Washington, DC 20001
www.newsguild.org

For a list of schools with accredited programs in journalism, contact:

Accrediting Council on Education in Journalism and Mass
    Communications
Stauffer-Flint Hall
1435 Jayhawk Boulevard
Lawrence, KS 66045
www.ku.edu/~acejmc

For general information about careers in journalism, contact:

Association for Education in Journalism and Mass
  Communication
234 Outlet Pointe Boulevard
Columbia, SC 29210
www.aejmc.org

National Newspaper Association
PO Box 7540
Columbia, MO 65205
www.nna.org

Names and locations of newspapers and a list of schools and
departments of journalism are published in the annual *Editor and
Publisher International Yearbook*, available in most public libraries
and newspaper offices.

Artists

For information on careers in the visual arts, contact:

Americans for the Arts
1000 Vermont Avenue NW, Sixth Floor
Washington, DC 20005
www.artsusa.org

American Craft Council
72 Spring Street, Sixth Floor
New York, NY 10012
www.craftcouncil.org

American Society of Interior Designers
608 Massachusetts Avenue NE
Washington, DC 20002
www.asid.org

Association for Living History, Farms and Agricultural
  Museums (ALHFAM)
8774 Route 45 NW
North Bloomfield, OH 44450
www.alhfam.org

Costume Society of America
PO Box 73
Earleville, MD 21919
www.costumesocietyamerica.com

The National Association of Schools of Art and Design
11250 Roger Bacon Drive, Suite 21
Reston, VA 20190
http://nasad.arts-accredit.org

National Assembly of State Arts Agencies
1029 Vermont Avenue NW, Second Floor
Washington, DC 20005
www.nasaa-arts.org

For information on careers in graphic design, contact:

The American Institute of Graphic Arts
164 Fifth Avenue
New York, NY 10010
www.aiga.org

For information on art careers in publishing, contact:

The Society of Illustrators
128 East Sixty-Third Street
New York, NY 10021
www.societyillustrators.org

The Society of Publication Designers
475 Park Avenue South, Suite 2200
New York, NY 10016
www.spd.org

For information on careers in medical illustration, contact:

The Association of Medical Illustrators
245 First Street, Suite 1800
Cambridge, MA 02142
www.medical-illustrators.org

For information on careers in scientific illustration, contact:

Guild of Natural Science Illustrators
PO Box 652, Ben Franklin Station
Washington, DC 20044
www.gnsi.org

Freelance Researchers

Additional information about careers in genealogy research can be obtained from the following sources:

National Genealogical Society
3108 Columbia Pike, Suite 300
Arlington, VA 22204
www.ngsgenealogy.org

Family History Library
35 North West Temple Street
Salt Lake City, UT 84150
www.familysearch.org

Board for Certification of Genealogists
PO Box 14291
Washington, DC 20004
www.bcgcertification.org

Association of Professional Genealogists
PO Box 350998
Westminster, CO 80035
www.apgen.org

Institute of Genealogy and Historical Research
Samford University
800 Lakeshore Drive
Birmingham, AL 35229
www.samford.edu/schools/ighr

Archivists

Additional information about careers for archivists can be obtained from the following sources:

Association of Canadian Archivists
PO Box 2596, Station D
Ottawa, ON K1P 5W6
Canada
www.archivists.ca

Library and Archives Canada
395 Wellington Street
Ottawa, ON K1A 0N4
Canada
www.collectionscanada.ca

U.S. National Archives and Records Administration
8601 Adelphi Road
College Park, MD 20740
www.archives.gov

Society of American Archivists
527 South Wells Street, Fifth Floor
Chicago, IL 60607
www.archivists.org

Computer Professionals

Further information about computer careers is available from:

Association for Computing Machinery
1515 Broadway
New York, NY 10036
www.acm.org

Information about certification as a computer professional is available from:

Institute for the Certification of Computer Professionals
2350 East Devon Avenue, Suite 115
Des Plaines, IL 60018
www.iccp.org

Information about certification as a Certified Quality Analyst is available from:

Quality Assurance Institute
Windsor at Metro Center
2101 Park Center Drive, Suite 200
Orlando, FL 32835
www.qaiusa.com

State employment service offices can provide information about job openings for computer programmers. Also check with your city's chamber of commerce for information on the area's largest employers.

Security Guards

Further information about work opportunities for guards is available from local employers and state employment service offices. Information about job opportunities, training, and links to other helpful resources is available from:

Security Jobs Network
41 West Lee Highway, Suite 59–108
Warrenton, VA 20186
www.securityjobs.net

Forest Rangers

For information about forestry careers and a list of forestry schools, contact:

Society of American Foresters
5400 Grosvenor Lane
Bethesda, MD 20814
www.safnet.org

For additional information about government forestry careers, contact:

USDA Forest Service
1400 Independence Avenue SW
Washington, DC 20250
www.fs.fed.us

For information about career in range management as well as a list of schools offering training, contact:

Society for Range Management
445 Union Boulevard, Suite 230
Lakewood, CO 80228
www.rangelands.org

For information about a career in soil conservation, contact:

Soil and Water Conservation Society
945 Southwest Ankeny Road
Ankeny, IA 50021
www.swcs.org

For information about work as a park ranger, contact the nearest regional office of the Forest Service:

Alaska Region
Forest Service
PO Box 21628
Juneau, AK 99802

Eastern Region
Forest Service
626 East Wisconsin Avenue
Milwaukee, WI 53202

Intermountain Region
Forest Service
324 Twenty-Fifth Street
Ogden, UT 84401

Northern Region
Forest Service
Federal Building
200 East Broadway
PO Box 7669
Missoula, MT 59807

Pacific Northwest Region
Forest Service
333 SW First Avenue
PO Box 3623
Portland, OR 97208

Pacific Southwest Region
Forest Service
1323 Club Drive
Vallejo, CA 94592

Rocky Mountain Region
Forest Service
740 Simms Street
Golden, CO 80401

Southern Region
Forest Service
1720 Peachtree Street, Suite 760S
Atlanta, GA 30309

Southwest Region
Forest Service
333 Broadway SE
Albuquerque, NM 87102

Mail Carriers

Local post offices and state employment service offices can supply details about entrance examinations and specific employment opportunities for postal clerks and mail carriers. Information is also available online at:

United States Postal Service
www.usps.com

About the Author

● ●

A full-time writer of career books, Blythe Camenson works hard to help job seekers make educated choices. She firmly believes that with enough information, readers can find long-term, satisfying careers. To that end, she researches traditional as well as unusual occupations, talking to a variety of professionals about what their jobs are really like. In all of her books she includes firsthand accounts from people who can reveal what to expect in each occupation.

Blythe Camenson was educated in Boston, earning her B.A. in English and psychology from the University of Massachusetts and her M.Ed. in counseling from Northeastern University.

In addition to *Careers for Introverts*, she has written more than two dozen books for McGraw-Hill.